M.A. Buth

Gold from Scrap

Revised Edition

24/4/2023

Be careful when handling chemicals.
Always wear protective clothes and
protect your eyes with glasses.
Don´t let family or other people near you
inhale fumes from chemicals.
Work outside if fumes are emitted, never
inside rooms.

Prologue

According to the United Nations Environmental Programme (UNEP), small-scale gold mining provides income for around 100 million people worldwide. The number of individuals who make a living from the precious metals found in everyday products is not precisely known, but it continues to grow daily.

This growth is driven not only by the rising prices of gold and other noble metals, but also by the increasing supply of precious scrap materials. The modern industrial society uses a wide range of precious metals in everyday products, which eventually reach the end of their life cycle. However, these metals can be recycled indefinitely, making it possible to extract value from discarded items.

Many sources of rare and precious metals remain undiscovered, with valuable materials being discarded daily. If done correctly, gold scrapping poses no harm to the environment or the people involved. The process typically involves mechanically dismantling materials, sorting, and concentrating the scrap, resulting in a higher value product than the original mixture of materials. This concentrated scrap can then be converted into cash, traded, or further refined.

The number of people participating in urban gold hunting is steadily increasing, as it offers a legal and independent means of improving one's income.

Fellow Preppers out there: It is smart to have **books in a printed form**. You know why....

About this book

In this book, I have focused on the many individuals who seek to improve their lives through hard work and independent labor. Although I cannot promise that anyone will make a fortune or become a millionaire overnight with scrap gold, the knowledge gained from this book will open doors and provide opportunities for those with minimal resources to earn extra income, often from the comfort of their homes.

I have intentionally kept this book simple, both in language and methods. While there are plenty of resources available for sophisticated gold miners, this book is designed to be accessible and affordable for those with limited means. As such, it is concise and less elaborate.

No matter where you live - be it Los Angeles, Moscow, Mexico City, Bangladesh, Cairo, Manila, or anywhere else in the world - this urban mining survival handbook is here to help you navigate the modern urban jungle and succeed in your endeavors.

Update: A decade after its initial publication, I have carefully revised and updated this book using a combination of AI tools and manual labor. Enjoy!

Marcel Alexander Buth, April 2023
Author

Table of contents

Buying gold scrap

Try to avoid purchasing **dedicated** gold scrap. The labor required to recover and concentrate the material is your profit, and spending money on it will only reduce that profit. Be patient and wait for other opportunities instead of making hasty purchases.

Your invested money may be tied up for a long time since gold scrapping is not a fast business. It could take months before you see any returns. This book is intended for newcomers, small businesses, and individuals in economically challenging situations. As long as there is enough free gold scrap that requires only labor and time, these sources should always be prioritized.

The internet provides various opportunities for scrap buyers, but be cautious. Well-known gold scrap items like computer parts are often overpriced, especially in online auctions. These deals are typically only profitable for traders who can buy, resell, or refine the materials with a small margin, making them unsuitable for the average recoverer.

There are always gold scrappers willing to trade their materials, possibly because they cannot obtain enough to process it profitably or simply do not know how to do so. Aim to trade materials instead of purchasing them to maximize your potential profits.

Your regional gold market

Flow of material

As material flows through the process, it becomes increasingly concentrated and accumulated at each stage, while the number of participants at each level decreases. At the final stage, only a handful of large refiners exist worldwide. These refiners are willing to buy from anyone, but they typically require a large quantity of material and will only pay after the batch has been processed – which may take months.

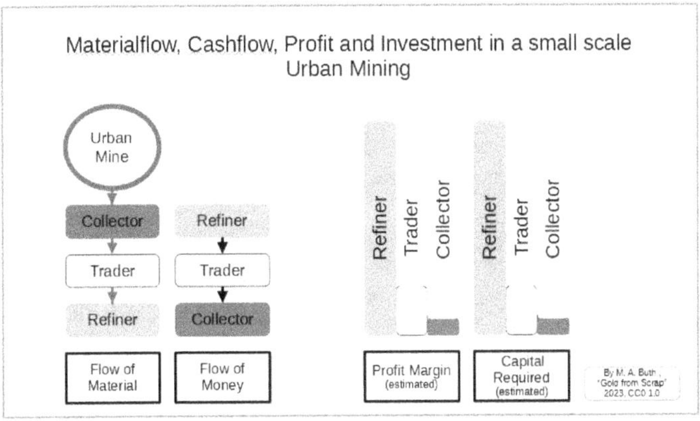

So, what is your position in the chain of material flow, and who is this book intended for?

The first stage of urban mining involves collecting base materials such as broken computers, notebooks, mobile phones, car parts, and household goods. You may collect your own materials or rely on others, such as scrapyards or car shops, to supply you with base materials.

The next stage involves the recoverer, which is the role this book primarily focuses on and recommends for beginners. The recoverer's job is to separate the materials into valuable and worthless parts. In other words, they act as both a concentrator and a sorter.
Once a recoverer has sorted enough material of one kind, they will either sell it to a trader or refiner, or attempt to refine it themselves. Start with what is easiest for you in the beginning. If collecting can be done quickly and easily, begin at that level. If you have access to large quantities of scrap already – perhaps even own a scrap yard or a business with a constant stream of scrap coming in – you can start recovering right away.

Traders are specialized middlemen in this business. They provide collectors and recoverers with cash, hold and accumulate precious scrap until there is enough to be processed by a refiner, and then sell or have it toll refined (refining someone's material for a fixed commission). Traders need what collectors and recoverers often lack: capital. They also face certain risks, such as precious metal price drops and low yields.

Trading and recovering often go hand in hand. The goal is to accumulate as much material as possible to ensure that the refining stage is profitable. Urban mining is all about quantity.

Some large traders may appear as if they were refineries, but all they do is buy materials, collect them, and then send them to a large refinery.
Their buying price will only be 5% - 10% of the true value of your gold scrap. However, they pay out quickly, which can sometimes be a decisive factor.

To overcome the trader barrier, start thinking of 100 kg to 1 ton as a minimum for moving on to the next step. It may take months or even years to amass this amount of material, but once it is there, the capitalization of the material begins. As long as precious metal prices remain high or continue to rise, this is the best strategy.

Another smart way to overcome the trader barrier is to collaborate with other gold scrappers and combine your scrap materials. You will need to ensure that everyone contributes a fair share, but the advantages are significant. With several hundred kilograms of material, you can approach large refiners directly. If they work honestly, you can receive up to 90% of the value from your scrap. It may take several weeks to see that money, but that's how the business works. Gold scrapping is not an ideal job for those who need daily payment; instead, it is a secondary opportunity for people who can afford to wait.

There is no fast and easy money for honest, hard-working people in this world.

Golden rules

If you can see gold, then there is gold:
Avoid pursuing gold in objects where it is not visible. If there is enough gold worth collecting, you will be able to see it with the naked eye. If you are unsure, break the object apart. If you still don't see any gold inside, forget about it.

Stay focused:
Do not attempt to follow more than 2-3 scrapping projects at once. Success in this business is a matter of quantity. If you pursue too many different projects, you won't achieve your goals in a timely manner. If your focus is gold, stick with gold; if it's silver, concentrate on silver. Don't waste time and effort on materials that are not your primary objective.

Cherry-picking:
When you acquire new material, select the part that best suits your needs and sell or trade the rest. Don't bother with low-grade material, as it will only distract you. Always adhere to the 80:20 rule.

Team up:
Find colleagues with whom you can exchange market information and scrap material. Establishing a network can be beneficial for both sharing knowledge and materials.

Concentrate:
Always strive to concentrate your material as densely as possible using the resources available to you. Sort different types of material to optimize the concentration and value of your scrap.

Collecting gold scrap

As a collector, your role is to go from house to house, asking people for their scrap. You don't pay for the scrap, as you are helping them keep their homes clean by removing unwanted items.

Keep a sharp eye out for items that have value, particularly those mentioned in this book, such as old computers, electronics, CDs, mobile phones, old glasses and watches, and gold-plated broken glassware. While collecting scrap might not be a highly regarded profession, it provides a starting point for those in need of material to work with and offers an opportunity to begin building an income.

A vehicle could help transport larger objects. It should be inexpensive and not incur additional costs. Larger vehicles can be rented as needed for specific occasions, and a storage space for the material should be available, preferably without monthly fees.

Remember to keep a low profile!

However, even without a vehicle, a backpack or an old sack can get the job done. Always stay focused on collecting small items with high value, rather than large, heavy items with little value.

Set up collection boxes for the items mentioned in this book. Look for shops, gas stations, and other locations where you can place simple cardboard or plastic boxes. Provide information about the collection, letting people know it's a clean and safe way to dispose of items like batteries.

Alternatively, make arrangements with shop owners so they can set items aside, allowing you to collect them every month or so.

Build a network of shops, factories, hospitals, and other sources that can supply you with a steady stream of raw material. Collect this material, remove non-valuable parts (concentrating), and begin recovering, refining, or reselling once you have accumulated enough to bring to market.

Needless to say, it is smarter to collect your material as "scrap" rather than as "gold scrap." The author recalls a case where a scrap collector arrived to pick up some aluminum in a Porsche, wearing a heavy gold chain around his neck. Unsurprisingly, the scrap was not given to him for free. Such a presentation raises suspicion about how much money one can make with old metal scrap. So, maintain a low profile and stay modest, and people will be more willing to give away their surplus items. Don't label your gold scrap as "gold scrap," or there won't be much to collect from someone who previously considered it worthless trash.

After collecting comes storage. As mentioned in the "golden" rules, try to **concentrate** material as much as possible, which will also require less storage space.

This approach reduces the risk of theft and other forms of loss, and keeps curious questioners at bay. The significant advantage of hunting for precious metals is that a few kilograms can be worth more than several tons of steel or other scrap metal. The value of 1 kg of gold equals 50 kg of silver, which in turn equals almost 800 kg of copper. So stick with rule number one: Stay focused. Don't become a clutterer. Sell or discard any material that is not precious metal!

Recovering gold scrap

Recovering is the part of the business that can be done at home. It allows the whole family to contribute to the result. For the most part, it involves dismantling and sorting items. In addition to precious metals, there may be other metals like copper and brass worth collecting and then turning in at the scrap yard.

Recovering requires no chemicals or complicated technology. The basic tools include pliers, knives, and other tools that can be found in any household or easily improvised. The objective of the recovering process is to sort, concentrate, and accumulate material until it reaches the "critical mass."

After reaching critical mass, sell, trade, or chemically process the material for pure gold or silver.. So, recovering means accumulating material for several months or even years, with payment coming after a long period. Recovering requires patience and endurance.It's not daily pay but accumulating savings for a later payou The good news is that this "savings" only requires time and labor, not money.

Nevertheless, recovering gold from everyday objects can be a profitable business if done correctly and typical mistakes are avoided. An average ton of electronic waste contains 100 times more gold than a ton of ore from a South African gold mine (4 g per ton vs 400 g/t!).

This doesn't even account for additional precious metals like silver, palladium, or platinum. Furthermore, a ton of electronic waste is made up of about 70% copper, which alone sells for about 5,000 to 7,000 USD today.

The challenge lies not in obtaining raw materials, but in extracting the precious metals from them with minimal effort. This book can be your first step in discovering where to look and how to proceed. Secondary steps will follow as experience and knowledge grow. Until then, collect and concentrate the material!

Tools

In order to successfully find, identify and recover gold and other precious metals, you should have some tools on you.

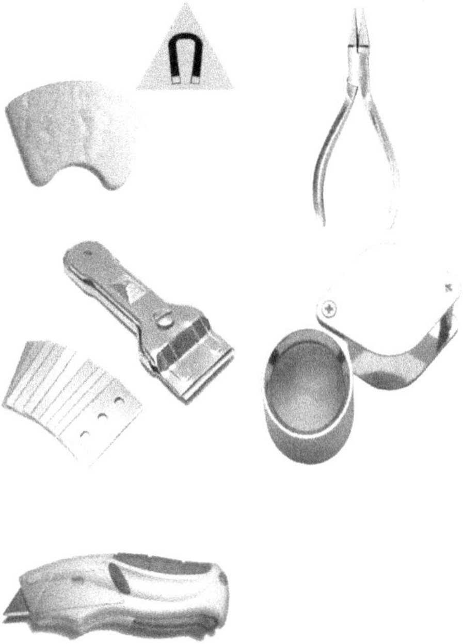

Neodymium magnet

Neodymium magnets are the strongest magnets known. This tool will be your companion from now on. It will help you determine whether a material contains certain base metals or not, and how high the precious metal content may be.

It will also assist you in separating mixed materials. Additionally, in one application, it will help you make money. You can obtain neodymium magnets from old hard disks. Open one, and you will find two of them inside.

Pliers

It would be beneficial to have a set of 2-3 different pliers on hand.

Razor blade

Some razor blades will help you in certain cases to scrape off the valuable material from a base material.

Magnifying glass

A magnifying glass will help you in many cases to determine if a material is solid gold or just gold plated, among other things.

Cutting knife

This knife is needed to cut out electronic components from circuit boards.

Gold from CDs

A CD, or Compact Disc, is a round, 12 cm diameter flat disc that can hold data such as music, video, or information. There are two basic types of CDs: CDs that can be written by a user – called CD-R for CD rewritable - and CDs that are manufactured in large series by special printing machines. The CD consists of a plastic layer, a thin metal layer that holds the data, and a protective coating on top. The plastic itself is already valuable and can be collected and later resold. The metal layer of normal mass-produced CDs consists of aluminum. The recovery of the precious metals from these types of CDs is not economical. The metal layer of CD-Rs, between the coating and the plastic, is made either of pure silver or pure gold. Unfortunately, many brands have been gold-colored and even carry gold in their product name, though they only have a silver layer. CD-Rs with a gold layer can often be distinguished by their cyan green or deep blue color on the backside.

To get to that precious metal, follow the instructions described here:

Step 1: Use a razor blade and carefully scratch one radial line from the center of the disc to the outer area.

Step 2: Take the razor blade and carefully begin to insert it into the small gap between the coating and the disc that you just created. Gently lift the coating up.

Step 3: Start to rotate the disc and remove the entire coating, along with the metal layer. You will now have one transparent disc and the coating separately.

Collect the remains for future recovery. Don't mix gold and silver. The same procedure can be used for other types of CDs, such as CD-RW.

As an alternative, the CD-R can be cooked in hot AP, which is a mix of HCl and H_2O_2 at a 1:3 ratio. Once the solution reaches 50°C, the gold coating will dissolve.

Another way is to place the CD-Rs in Aqua Regia. It will take up to 1 day before the chlorine from the Aqua Regia has reached into the middle layer and dissolved the gold.
This procedure is not recommended because of the relatively high amount of strong acids required.
A third way is to use an electrolytic process and deplate the discs with an electrolytic cell. It does not seem very practical, but it has been demonstrated that it can be done.
The author recommends the mechanical removal of the gold layer as the first step. This will greatly reduce the amount of chemicals needed to dissolve the gold in the next step.
An intermediate incineration will be helpful in this regard as well.
The plastic from the CD is called Macrolon® and sells for around 600 US$ per ton. So it is worth collecting as well.

Facts:
One disc contains around 15mg to 25mg of silver or gold. That means, 40 to 60 discs make up for one gram of gold or silver.
The author found 400 gold-plated CD-Rs in a batch of 1 ton (=1000 kg). That makes 10g of gold per ton. A CD weighs approximately 100g.
In that ton, there were also around 2000 CD-Rs that were silver-plated, representing 50g of silver.

Gold from eye wear

Glasses often contain gold or even platinum.
The type of material here is called gold-filled. In the USA, the quality of gold-filled is defined by the Federal Trade Commission.
You can recognize the amount of gold that is in the metal by looking at the numbers that are embossed in them. First of all, they should be marked as GF or gold-filled.
Gold-filled is a carat gold content per unit of weight. So numbers such as 1/10, 1/20,1/50, 1/100 mean 10%, 5% , 2%, and 1% karat gold by total weight of the frame.
Remove the glasses and all parts that are non-metal.
Use some pliers to cut the frame into handy pieces. If they are hollow and have further parts inside, check them for value.
It is advisable to incinerate the pieces prior to chemical treatment, to ensure that all organic material has been removed.
Use 400°C to 600°C heat for several minutes to do that.
Processing gold-filled material is not so easy with small-scale means, because it will take a lot of nitric acid to remove all unwanted metals prior to getting to the noble metals. So the best suggestion is to collect as much as possible and sell it for a good price.

Gold from glassware

Gold-plated glassware is popular in many countries. There are gold-plated tea glasses, coffee cups, beer mugs, and much more.

Most of the glassware that looks as if it was gold-plated actually is gold-plated. Only the thickness of the gold plating can vary tremendously.
Since there is no other metal involved in recovering gold-plated glassware, the gold can be dissolved directly by all common methods.

First, reduce the surface of the glassware to the gold-plated areas, which means you will have to break them apart. This will reduce the amount of chemicals needed for the next steps.
One popular way is to put the pieces in HCl, then drop Clorox/bleach on them. The gold will then dissolve and drop into the HCl where it later can be precipitated very easily, for instance, with copper since there are no other metals involved.
The plating can also be dissolved using Aqua Regia directly.

Gold from jeweleries

Harvesting gold-plated parts from watches and their bracelets is quite popular in some regions of the world. The material is called GF for gold filled and is regulated by the Federal Trade Commission in the United States. Gold-filled jewelry, also known as "rolled gold" or "rolled gold plate," consists of a solid layer of gold bonded with heat and pressure to a base metal, such as brass.

Some high-quality gold-filled pieces have the same appearance as 14 karat (58%) gold. In the USA, the quality of gold filled is defined by the Federal Trade Commission. If the gold layer is 10 kt fineness, the minimum layer of karat gold in an item stamped GF must equal at least 1/10 the weight of the total item.

If the gold layer is 12 kt or higher, the minimum layer of karat gold in an item stamped GF must equal at least 1/20 the weight of the total item. The most common stamps found on gold-filled jewelry are 1/20 12kt GF, 1/20 14kt GF, and 1/10 10kt. Sterling silver bases are less common in today's pricier products.

"Double clad" gold-filled sheet is produced with 1/2 the thickness of gold on each side. 1/20 14Kt double-clad gold-filled has a layer on each side of 1/40th 14Kt, making the total gold content 1/20. The thinner layer on each side does not wear as well as single-clad gold-filled.

The Federal Trade Commission allows the use of "Rolled Gold Plate" or "R.G.P." on items with lower thicknesses of gold than are required for "gold-filled." A 12 kt gold layer that is 1/60 the weight of the total item is designated as 1/60 12kt RGP. However, this lower quality does not wear as well as gold-filled items.

One problem for later recovery is the stainless steel used in many watches alongside the gold. It is difficult to dissolve and requires a lot of acid, making it uneconomical in some cases. Sometimes watches are marked with a carat number and a factor. To obtain the percentage of the 24-carat gold used on the watch, all non-precious metal parts, such as glasses, stainless steel parts, and other non-gold parts, must be removed, especially the stainless steel springs inside the watchband elements.

The formula for calculating the overall gold percentage is: factor x carat/24 x 100 = total gold percentage. For example, if a watchband carries the numbers 1/10 and 14k, that would mean 1/10 x 14/24 x 100 = 4.17%. Assuming the watchband weighs 100g, the total amount of pure gold in that band is 4.17g. However, the gold in these parts is plated and, therefore, only present on the surface. Much gold may have worn off with years of watch use.

Another way to concentrate the gold is to rub it off using a file or other abrasive methods.

It is recommended to heat the parts, such as top caps and watch cases, to red prior to further processing to remove unwanted material. The gold-plated parts can then only be dissolved by a strong solution like Aqua Regia since by far most of the material is base metal or deplated using an electrolytic (sulfuric) cell.

Gold from diabetes test strips etc.

Many everyday objects have gold-plated areas on them, and a rather unexpected field of recovery is the one-way test strips from diabetes testers and other one-way medical testing tools. If one can obtain a large number of these test strips, the gold on them can be easily recovered.

Hospitals are a significant source of these strips, and one may know someone who works there or can set up collecting boxes for used strips.

One kilogram of these test strips yields only around 1-2 grams of gold, which may not seem like much. However, considering how easy it is to collect these strips, it can be worth the effort. These gold-plated fields on the test strips are necessary to achieve accurate measuring results. You can also look out for any one-way tests that may have a gold-plated area.

But here's a word of caution: since these test strips have been used and are contaminated with human blood, it is important to disinfect them properly using hot water and/or disinfectants such as isopropyl alcohol before handling them.

Otherwise, there is a risk of contracting diseases from dried blood on the strips.

After collecting and disinfecting the strips, simply cut away any parts that do not have gold on them to concentrate the gold. Another source of gold-on-plastic material is credit cards, payback cards, and any plastic cards that have a gold-plated area on them.

Another source of gold-plated material on plastic are SIM cards from mobile phones. To extract the gold, the plastic should be removed using a pair of scissors to cut away any non-gold portions. It is important to minimize the plastic content as much as possible to reduce chemical consumption and increase the final yield. An alternative way to separate the precious metal-containing chip from the rest of the material is to boil it in NaOH (lye) for about 30 minutes, which will cause the chips to separate from their carrier material and can then be processed individually.

If enough raw material has been collected, the standard procedure for obtaining pure gold can be followed. Since we do not expect any other metals to be involved and the plastic of the strips does not interfere with the reaction, the gold is dissolved using a gold-dissolving chemical and then precipitated.

If the material is grey, it could made of or contain palladium.

Gold from computers

There are two major sources of gold from IT hardware. First, it is the CPU, which is the main electronic component of a computer. It is a square object called a "chip," which has many gold-plated pins on the bottom. It is these pins that contain the most gold.

Secondly, there are add-on cards that are plugged into the sockets on the motherboard in a 90° orientation. These add-on cards have to interconnect with the motherboard, and they do so by using gold-plated contacts called "gold fingers."

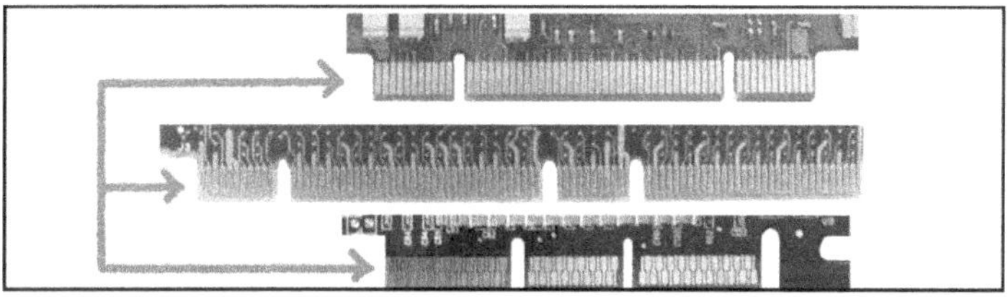

These gold fingers are the most profitable source of gold in a computer! They are very easy to discover, recover, and even transfer into pure gold. The plating of these gold fingers is very thick and is usually 20-24 karat gold.

So if one can get these add-on cards with these gold fingers, this is the best and most profitable source of gold in electronics. To remove the gold fingers from the add-on card, simply use some pliers and clip them off. The material now has a 1% gold ratio, which means 100 g of gold fingers will yield 1 g of fine gold!

It is the most concentrated and therefore richest source of gold in a computer. 1% is the maximum yield, while most other gold-plated components in a computer have a yield of 0.1-0.5%.

If a higher concentration is sought, one can use a tool like a chisel and remove the individual gold-plated contacts one by one.

To do so, the chisel is used to pry up one corner of a gold plated contact. Then carefully and slowly wiggle the contact back and forth until it comes loose from the board. The removed contacts now have a +60% gold content. The rest will most likely be nickel, which is why those contacts will react to magnets despite being mainly made of gold.

The material now consists of metals only, so it could be melted without prior chemical treatment if desired, resulting in a low grade gold button.

There is more gold to be found in computers, but the goldfingers are the most profitable source of gold with a content that is 10 times higher than any other gold-plated component in a computer.

Gold in Chips and CPUs

The most popular gold source is the CPU of a computer. This is the biggest chip inside a computer. The amount of gold in such a microchip varies depending on the model from 0,1 g to 0,3 g per unit.

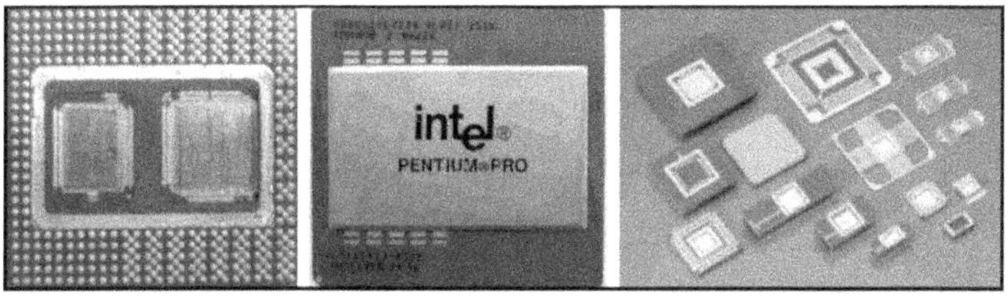

The larger the chip is and the more contact pins it has, the more gold can be expected.

CPUs yield not only gold but also silver, palladium, and rhodium. Most of the value is outside the CPU in the gold plated pins. Wherever possible try to remove those gold plated pins and collect them. This is by far the most part of the gold there is in a CPU.

The sockets, where the cards with the goldfingers were located at, also carry gold on their counterpart contacts. They can be removed mechanically with pliers, or using a heat gun, heating the boards from the backside and tapping on them until the solder melts and the gold plated contacts fall down.

The larger chips on the boards are also worth harvesting for their precious metals.

They may not be immediately visible, but they are there, hidden inside the usually black housing. We will discuss the removal and processing of these chips in the next chapter. The general rule of thumb is that the bigger the chips are, the more they are worth collecting.

Generally speaking, most contacts in a computer do have gold-plated areas on them. A visual inspection should confirm this. If there is visible gold on the tip of a contact, it is worth collecting. The rest of the material is mostly (+90%) copper, zinc, or nickel.

Older electronics have more precious metals than newer ones. With low gold and palladium prices in the 1980s-1990s, their usage was common, but as prices soared, they were replaced by cheaper base metals.

A magnet distinguishes cheap from precious metals in electronics; attracted components imply low value, while non-attracted ones suggest precious metals.

All in all, old computers are a rich source of precious metals today. Remember the golden rules and cherry-pick only the most valuable parts, which include:

- the CPU
- the goldfingers from expansion cards
- the memory sticks
- the larger chips on the board
- any easy-to-unsolder or break-out sockets
- the keyboard mylars

Head on to the next gold scrap fest and leave the rest to the vultures of the scrap yard!

Before you start a big mess with those electronic parts do some research!

Either you may sell them as they are to as specialized company or they may have a high value if they are still intact!

Some collectors pay high prices for vintage chips.

Also some industrial companies need those end-of-life components, which are no longer produced. Do some research on the internet, using the part number that should always be printed on top of these chips. Some old chips sell for hundreds of dollars if in working condition!

Gold from mobile phones

Mobile phones contain some gold, but not too much. Focus on the large gold-plated components on the board that you find inside a mobile phone.

Opening a mobile phone can be quite difficult, because many need special tool. Use bare force and take a hammer or else to smash the phone.

Take out the **SIM card**, it has gold plated contacts. The procedure and details have been described in this book a few chapters before.

Take out **battery contacts**, they are gold plated – both inside the mobile phone and at the battery pack.

Inside the mobile phone remove the **antenna jacket** and any component that is mounted on the board of the mobile phone and that look golden.

Discard and sell or trade the rest. The gold-plating of the board is very thin, even if it may look richly plated.

The small components, called **microchips** that are mounted on the board, also contain precious metals. Use a razor blade and cut them out. The procedure is shown in the next chapter. If they cannot be cut out use a heat gun and unsolder them with hot air.

Gold from microchips

Many electronic device contain so called microchips.

Most of them contain tiny amounts of gold, well hidden inside these packages at their center. Microchips come in countless forms, shapes, and colors, but they are all flat and usually black. Some have leads that are soldered to the board underneath their package, and these can be removed using a flat screwdriver or a chisel.

Another method is to apply heat, using a heat gun at around 400°C. The hot air will make the tin melt, and the components can be picked up. Alternatively, a simple hot plate can be used. Place the board on it and, as soon as the tin melts, slap it against a wall or a brick to make many components fall off.

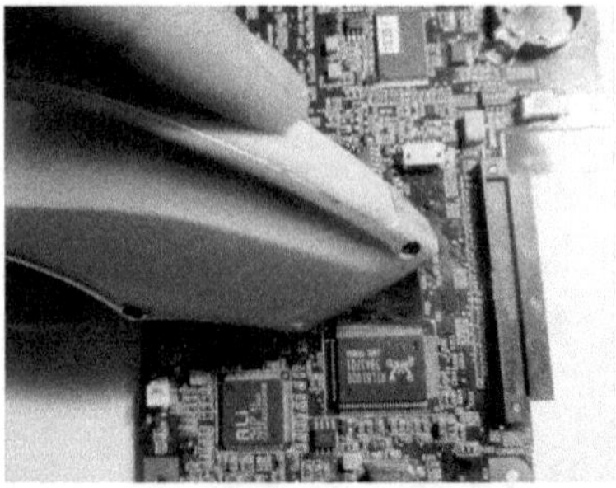

It is also a fast and clean way to use a sharp knife or a cutter knife to cut these chips off the board they were soldered on. Cut right through the leads or legs of those chips, but discard and remove those leads as they contain no value.

If you are planning to process this material by yourself or you have limited space for storage, you should concentrate the material. To further concentrate the material, cut off the edges of the chips. The gold is almost only in the very center of the flatpack. Use some pliers and chip off 1/3 of the outer area. Keep the remaining material as low-grade material for future use or sale, but focus on the center material as it contains the gold.

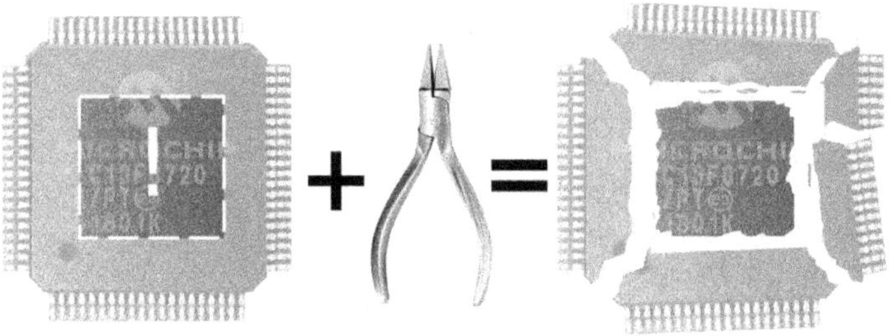

Collect at least 500 g to 1 kg of these chips.

Step 1:

Incinerate them, meaning put them in a vessel (an old can for instance) heat them inside an oven. Blow air into the vessel.

Have holes in the bottom of that vessel and blow fresh air into it, so that oxygen will reach the heated chips instead of the fire, which would only increase the heat. A temperature of 400°C to 600°C should be achieved and maintained.

Stay away from the fumes, as they can be harmful to your health.

After 5-10 minutes, the chips should be roasted and their color should have changed from black to white or red.

It is important to understand the difference between Incineration and Pyrolysis in this process!

Incineration means burning a material while adding oxygen, f.e. by blowing air into the fire while Pyrolysis means burning a material without adding extermal oxygen.

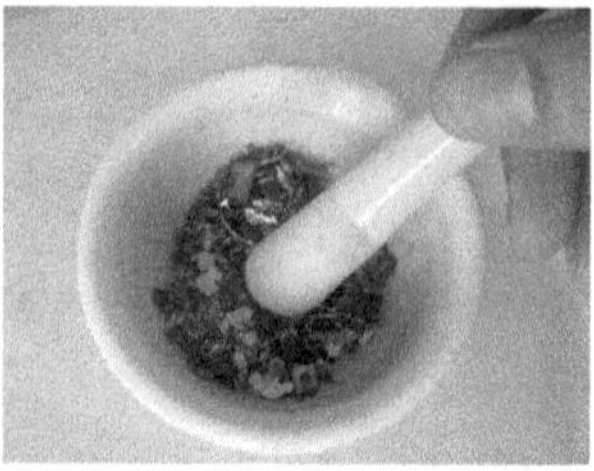

Step 2:

Let them cool down, then crunch them. Remove large pieces, that are either non-metal or aluminum.

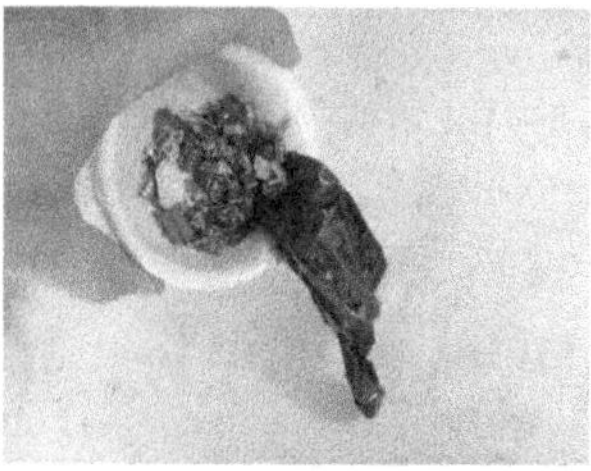

Step 3:

Add water to the material, siphon off the black-dirty water until it remains clear.

Step 4:

Use your neodymium magnet and remove all magnetic material from the chips. Collect it for later use. It may contain precious metals as well.

The first step in the recovery process is to remove any non-metallic material, such as glass and plastic, using a magnet to separate the metals from the waste. Then, use a furnace or kiln to melt down the remaining metals into one homogeneous mix. The gold wires will become visible in the molten mix and can be skimmed off with a scoop or tongs. It is important to use caution during this process, as molten metal can be dangerous if mishandled.

Once the gold wires have been collected, they can be further processed to remove any remaining impurities. One common method is to dissolve the gold in a mixture of nitric and hydrochloric acid, also known as aqua regia. This will separate the gold from any other metals in the wire. The gold can then be precipitated out of the solution using a reducing agent such as sodium metabisulfite.

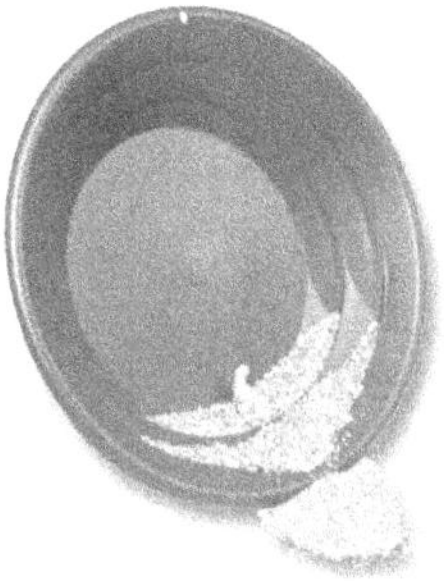

Step 5:

Use a gold pan and pan of anything that is not gold.

At this point the material could also be dissolved with Aqua Regia as an alternative.

1 kg of chips will yield around 1 g-2 g of gold average. There a chips that yield higher so up to 5 g gold per kilo raw material is possible.

The gold that you harvest from this method is solid and quite pure. Still there are other metals and non-metals in the mix. In case there is no refining abilities this mix may be melted without prior refining.

But, in order to obtain all precious metals involved it is necessary to dissolve the final material and drop the metals.

Expected precious metals are: Gold, silver, palladium, rhodium.

Silver from X-ray films etc

X-ray films from hospitals, labs and other medical facilities are made of a plastic layer, gelatine and silver oxide.

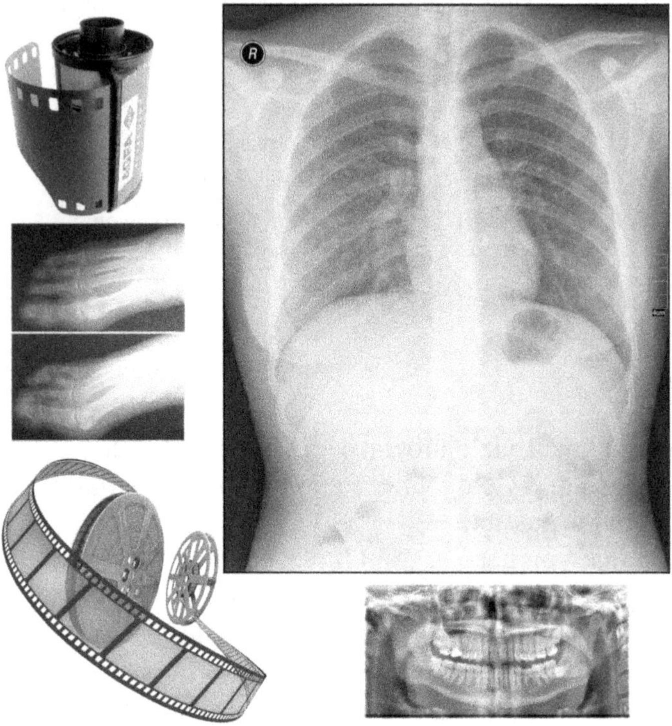

Just as with x-ray films, the same process can be used for negatives from old analog cameras and even old films from cinemas. The recovery process is the same for all of these materials.

Film types for recovery include analog cameras, dental x-rays, and cinema material. Organizations digitize film to prevent decomposition and ease access. Numerous raw material sources exist, like private households' old x-rays, so explore creatively.

In order to recover the silver, or silver oxide from the films, it is necessary to dissolve the gelatine, that holds the silver in place.
There are several ways, on how to do this generally speaking, any strong chemical cleaner, lye etc. will do the job. The gelatin is not very special and it will give in if a strong chemical is being used.

A very simple and cheap one is Chlorex ® (or Chlorox ® in some countries), or a similar chlorine-based household or toilet cleaner.

To clean x-ray films, dilute the cleaner with water at a ratio of around 1:5. Submerge the films in this diluted Chlorex® solution overnight or for a few hours. After that, it should be possible to wipe off the silver and glue residue.

Collect the wiped-off residue in a cloth or similar material. Rinse it carefully with water, making sure not to wash out fine silver particles. Let it dry and collect until there is at least 1 kg of material.

Sell the material as silver scrap or further process it by following these steps:

- Dissolve the dried material in dilute nitric acid (20%) and stir.
- Filter the solution through a cloth. The glue remains in the cloth while the dissolved silver passes through as silver nitrate.
- Add pure silver to the solution until no more silver dissolves. This means that the solution is now saturated.
- Add a large piece of pure copper or pure copper wire formed as a spiral to the silver nitrate solution.

Over time, pure 995 silver will precipitate out of the solution.

Silver from batteries

Some batteries are made of silver oxide and pure silver. It is the small ones that are used for watches, calculators, cameras etc.

We can identify them by their name which is printed on them. Try to collect old batteries from businesses that deal with those small batteries, such as watch shops or shops that sell hearing aids.

You can even set up a can in a store with a nice print and text wrapped around it, encouraging people to recycle batteries to help protect the environment. Or you may offer your services to replace empty batteries door-to-door, with non-silver replacement types for silver oxide batteries.

Get creative in finding ways to collect those little precious batteries.

Not all button batteries contain silver. In fact, there are three principal types of button batteries: Lithium, Manganese dioxide (MnO2) and silver oxide (Ag2O), used in watches, hearing aids, digital thermometers, cameras, computers, calculators, keyless car devices, iPods and more.

Lithium batteries can be easily recognized because they are very flat, like a coin, and have the letters "CR" followed by a number on the backside, along with the legend "LITHIUM 3V". These batteries do not contain silver, but you can recover the lithium.

All silver oxide batteries have a manufacturer's name, a number between 301 and 399, or the letters "SR" followed by a number between 43SW to 1130W.

It has been reported that around 300 g to 350 g of the 1 kg of collected used batteries are silver oxide, although this figure may vary. However, this makes this small business potentially profitable.

Silver oxide is found inside the shell of the batteries, so you must use pliers to open them. Don't worry, silver batteries are not likely to explode or release dangerous chemicals quickly.

For the recovery process, it is recommended to dissolve 250 g of crushed silver pellets from the button batteries in 1 liter of nitric acid. After about 30 minutes, all silver should be dissolved and the solution can be filtered using a cloth. The resulting solution will contain a mixture of zinc, silver, and mercury nitrate (AgNO3, ZnNO3, and HgNO3).

The next step should be the separation of the mercury nitrate. To do this, add common salt to the solution, and a white precipitant will appear, which is a mix of AgCl and HgCl. Stir the solution well, allow the solids to settle, and then decant the solution on top. Add NH4OH (ammonium hydroxide) to the solution until everything dissolves, and mercury will precipitate as a black powder as Hg(NH2)Cl.

Filter the liquid and keep the toxic black precipitant separate from the rest in a sealed container.
To the filtrated liquid, add HCl to re-precipitate the AgCl, forming the white clumps again, now free of mercury. You can then process it as the standard way by adding NaOH, washing, and adding Karo syrup, which will yield 0.999 silver.

List of button batteries that contain silver [1]:

Brand	CODE
PAKKO	From 301 to 399
SEIKO	SB-A5, SB-A6, SB-A8, SB-A9, SB-AB, SB-AC, SB-AE, SB-AF, SB-AG, SB-AH, SB-AJ, SB-AK, SB-AL, SB-AN, SB-AP SB-AR, SB-AS, SB-AT, SB-AU, SB-AW, SB-B1, SB-B8, SB-B9, SB-BK, SB-BL, SB-BN, SB-BP, SB-BS, SB-BU, SB-BW
SONY	From SR43SW to SR1130W
TOSHIBA	From SR43SW to SR1130W
PANASONIC	From SR43SW to SR1130W
SEIZAIKEN	From SR43SW to SR1130W
CITIZEN	280-01, 280-08, 280-13, 280-15, 280-17, 280-18, 280-24, 280-27, 280-28, 280-29, 280-30, 280-31, 280-34, 280-39, 280-41, 280-44, 280-45 ,280-46, 280-48, 280-51, 280-52, 280-53, 280-56, 280-58, 280-59, 280-60, 280-61, 280-66, 280-68, 280-70, 280-72, 280-73, 280-75, 280-77
DURACELL	From D301 to D399
ETA	From 301 to 399
ENERGIZER	From 301 to 399
EVEREADY	From 301 to 399
GP BATTERIES	From GB301 to GP399
RAYOVAC	From 301 to 399
RENATA	From 301 to 399
SWISEBAUCHERS	From SR43SW to SR1130W
MAWELL	From SR43SW to SR1130W
MALAM	From SR43SW to SR1130W
VARTA	From V301 to V399

This chapter contains information supplied by [1].

Silver from CDs and DVDs

The process of recovering gold from CD-Rs has been described before. The same procedure can be used for silver plated CD-Rs as well. However, recovering silver from writable DVDs (DVD-R) requires a bit more work.

Step 1: In order to get to the metallic layer the DVD has to be split. Take the razor blade and enter between the two layers.

Step 2: Start to split the two layers. One will be just transparent plastic and the other one will carry the metal.

To recover silver from DVD-Rs, the first step is to separate the two layers of the disc. This can be done using a razor blade or similar tool to carefully split the disc apart. Once separated, the very thin silver layer will be visible on one of the two parts of the disc.

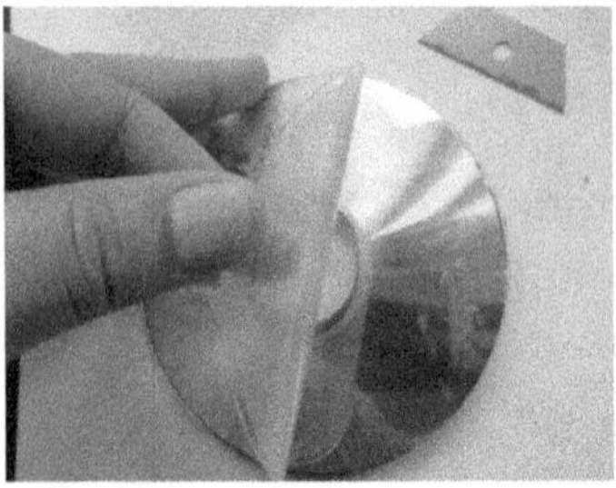

Step 3: Start tearing the thin, transparent foil away from the metal layer underneath.

Final stage: In the end the metal layer with either gold or silver on it is accessible.

This layer is too thin to be scraped off like with CDs, so the pure silver can only be collected by soaking the part with the silver layer in dilute nitric acid. If the layer is gold-plated, the gold can be recovered later using gold-dissolving chemicals.

Silver from solar panels

The most commonly used precious metals in solar modules are silver and sometimes gold.

Silver is used in the production of solar cells and makes up a significant portion of the cost of a solar module. The amount of silver used can vary depending on the specific design of the solar module, but it typically ranges from 15 to 30 grams per square meter of solar cell.

Gold is also used in some solar cells, particularly those used in space applications where reliability and durability are critical. However, the amount of gold used in solar cells is much lower than that of silver and typically ranges from just a few micrograms to a few milligrams per cell.

Discarded solar panels are an interesting upcoming recycling object. The traces that you can see on their surface, are silver-plated. There are developments in the industry, to replace the precious silver by other non-precious metals to make them cheaper.

But as of today this technology has not entered the market yet. Chances are good that if you get your hands on some broken panels, they are coated with silver. It will not be very much but you may get them for free. Check your scrap yard, although that may be already to late to get them for a good bargain. Keeps your eyes open after storms or other events that will render solar panels broken. As said, the silver layer may be thin and silver is not very expensive, but it may pay off to watch out for this source of silver.

Practical steps:
Solar panels defines an array of multiple solar cells connected by silver coated copper traces. The majority of precious metals should be found within the cells. In recovering silver from solar cells, we can compare two methods that involve two steps each. The first step is preparing the material, followed by applying acid.

The first method involves grinding the cells into a fine powder, followed by applying nitric acid to dissolve both copper and silver. This method is highly efficient and can recover a high yield of precious metals in a shorter time due to the large surface area of the powder that allows for fast acid dissolution.

The second method involves crushing the cells and then using nitric acid to dissolve both copper and silver. This can yield the same amount of precious metals as the first method, but it takes longer for the acid to creep through the cracks in the glass cover to reach the metal.

Expect to produce much more chemical waste, as all the material that has not been dismantled will be either covered with acid or will need to be washed off.

The image shows a stack of dismantled solar cells. Size, shape and appearance may vary.

In summary, while the second method is simpler and requires less specialized equipment, the yield of precious metals may take longer to achieve. On the other hand, the first method can recover a high yield of precious metals in a shorter amount of time due to the increased surface area. The choice of which method to use depends on the specific needs and circumstances of the recovery process.

The cleanest method involves dismantling solar panels, separating metal and non-metal fractions, concentrating materials, and detaching cells. Then, grind cells and dissolve the metal fraction.

The most environmentally friendly approach, however, is to select the undamaged cells. Since each cell operates independently, they can be reused or resold without requiring any chemical processing.

Pros and cons of the two methods to recover silver from solar cells

Method 1:

Pros:

- Ground powder offers a larger reaction surface, resulting in fast and complete dissolution.

Cons:

- Grinding requires investment in tools.
- Grinding tools will wear over time and have to be replaced.
- Grinding requires energy.

Method 2:

Pros:

- It is cheap to perform.
- No special tools needed.
- Manually cracking the glass surface is a fast process.

Cons:

- It requires more acid as it will also cover parts of the cell that are not involved in the process.
- The waste generated will be much more
- It will take longer to recover the silver.

Silver and Palladium from e-cars

Modern electric cars contain quite a large amount of precious metals, mostly in their battery systems. Expect to find silver, gold, and palladium. The amount might be significant, considering the high prices for these materials. This is a relatively new field, and you could be one of the first to benefit. All batteries break down sooner or later, and even if a car battery has caught fire, the precious metals are still there. They can resist temperatures above 1000°C without melting down.

This what ChatGPT had to say about precious metals in e-car batteries:

The precious metals in electric car batteries serve different purposes:

- Silver is often used as a conductor in the battery's electrodes and electrical connections.

- Gold is used in small amounts as a corrosion-resistant coating for electrical contacts.

- Palladium is used as a catalyst in the cathode of the battery to speed up the chemical reaction that produces electricity.

While the amount of these precious metals in each electric car battery may not be large, the overall demand for electric vehicles has been growing rapidly, and this has resulted in increased demand for these materials.

As the text suggests, recycling electric car batteries could potentially yield significant amounts of these precious metals, which could be an attractive opportunity for those interested in this field.

Electric cars are a rapidly advancing technology, and there is much to explore and experiment with regarding the recovery of precious metals from them. For now, it is expected that the majority of these valuable metals are located in either the battery or the electric drive system, with the main component being the electric

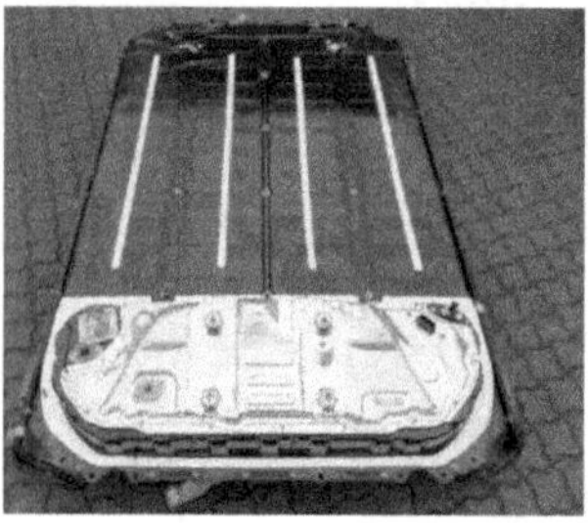

motors. It is important to watch out for these components in wrecked or broken cars, and when there is little information available, start gathering data.

As an example, let's consider the lithium battery and electric drive (also known as the electric motor) from a Tesla car, to give you an idea of what these objects look like. It's worth noting that appearance, size, and shape may vary from car to car. Left side battery, right image a motor.

Silver and palladium from relays

The magnetic field generated by passing an electric current through the coil of a relay activates the armature, which in turn causes the movable contact(s) to either make or break a connection with a fixed contact. Relays are commonly used in electronic circuits to control a wide variety of electrical devices, such as motors, lights, and solenoids. The design and construction of relays can vary widely depending on their intended use, with some relays incorporating multiple contacts or specialized features such as latching mechanisms or delay circuits.

If the set of contacts was closed when the relay was de-energized, then the movement opens the contacts and breaks the connection, and vice versa if the contacts were open. When the current to the coil is switched off, the armature is returned by a force, approximately half as strong as the magnetic force, to its relaxed position.
Relays come in many shapes and sizes. Some of them are not suited for recovering precious metals at all. The type of value are the ones, that give the typical clacking sound when operating. We find them in older cars and other vehicles like ships and boats, planes or large machines. The more power a relay has to switch, the more massive the precious metal contacts must be, to be able to transfer the energy.

Another source for relays are ancient telephone systems as well as antique computer hardware from the 1960s to 1970s.

The point of interest are the contacts that close a circuit. They are usually made of solid silver or palladium, even platinum sometimes. So this part of the relay is very precious and it is also often quite large. All it takes is some brute force to hammer open the case and then some pliers to cut away that precious part of this electronic component. Here are just some samples on how relays may look and where the precious metal contact can be found.

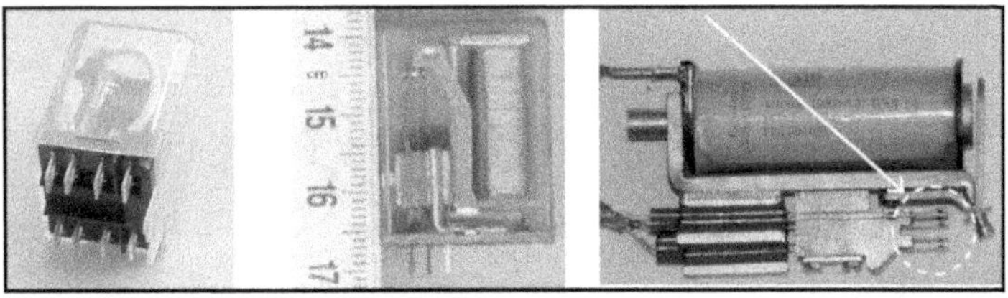

The contacts should just be pinched off and collected. The remaining metal is a copper coil plus some low value scrap.

Platinum from spark plugs

Some **center electrodes** of spark plugs are plated with platinum, silver and/or iridium on a copper core. This is the case if the engine gets very hot or is high powered.

AUTOMOBILE SPARK PLUG

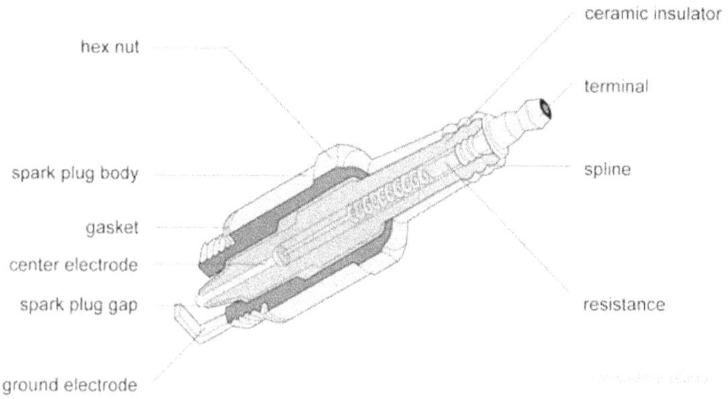

The development of noble metal high-temperature electrodes, using metals such as yttrium, iridium, tungsten, or palladium, as well as the relatively high-value platinum, silver, or gold, allows for the use of a smaller center wire that has sharper edges but will not melt or corrode away. The side or ground electrode is made from high-nickel steel and is either welded or hot-forged to the side of the metal shell. By examining the spark plug, you can identify the iridium center electrode, which is much thinner than a normal nickel-base electrode. To extract the valuable metal, use a hammer to smash the ceramic body of the spark plug. Remove the center electrode and store it for later use.

We can also differentiate between spark plugs containing precious metals and those without by using a strong magnet. Since nickel is magnetic, it will be easy to identify the spark plugs with precious metals. Collect the inner electrodes from these spark plugs for later processing.

Remember that spark plus can be found not only in cars, but also in trucks, boats, planes and other engines.

Platinum & palladium from cats

Almost all cars do have a catalytic converter, or short "cat". This cat is part of the exhaust. The picture shows a catalytic converter on a 1996 Dodge Ram van just as an example. Appearance, shape or size may vary.

The cat, short for catalytic converter, is usually located close to the engine and connects to the exhaust on the other side. It contains precious metals such as platinum, palladium, and rhodium which are used as catalysts to convert harmful gases into less harmful ones.

These metals can either be in the form of many small pellets or a honeycomb-like structure.

In order to recover the precious metals from the catalytic converter, it has to be opened, preferably with an angle grinder, also known as a side grinder or disc grinder. The process should be done with caution as the cat contains harmful substances such as lead and arsenic. It is recommended to wear a mask and gloves while handling the device.

Commonly found precious metals are: palladium, platinum and/or rhodium. The amounts vary from 2-6 g per cat.

The recovery process should start by opening the catalytic converter with an appropriate tool and collecting the internal cell, whether it consists of pellets or honeycomb structures.

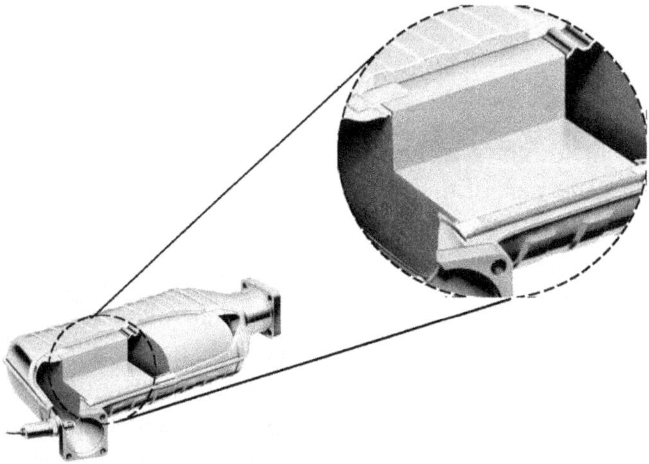

There are several ways to remove the precious metals from those catalytic structures, but it should be taken into account that the cells have a very large surface area and therefore the metals require a longer period of time to completely dissolve from them.

They can either be boiled in hot HCl, Aqua Regia, or HCl + Cl for several hours or even days.

The resulting liquid must then be filtered, and the precious metals must be precipitated.

Separating palladium from platinum is difficult and requires good knowledge of the procedure and the appropriate equipment, so it may be an option to sell or trade the cells as they are and stick with scrap that is easier to handle.

How to get a fair price

Transparency in the market is key to receiving fair prices for your work. Utilize technology to find out how much buyers from other locations are paying for your gold scrap. Connect with other gold scrappers from abroad or in another town to exchange knowledge of prices and conditions.

- Cooperation is better than competition.
- Utilize the internet, phone, or any means necessary to obtain information about a fair price.
- Do not depend on a single buyer!
- After preparing yourself, compare conditions between several buyers and choose the best deal.

If you have access to the internet, visit websites that deal with this type of scrap and ask about the current market price for your material. Be sure to describe your material as thoroughly as possible and consider uploading photos if you can.

More urban mining

These are short ideas for potential sources of precious metals or even money.
Now your neodymium magnet plays a major role.

Harvesting a large city for values

Wherever there are people, they tend to lose things, and you can use your magnet to find those lost items. You can search in spots where many people pass by or have to wait, as the chance of finding jewelry or money is high in those places. However, constantly bending down and searching may not be feasible or desirable, so here is a discreet trick to help you search the ground.
Tie your neodymium magnet to a cord and have it run down your leg inside your pants so that the magnet can touch the ground unseen and pick up magnetic objects. Then, as you retrace the cord through your pockets, you can collect any coins, rings, or other items you find without drawing attention to yourself. Alternatively, you can mount a magnet directly underneath your shoe. You'll need to experiment with both setups since neodymium magnets are very strong, and it may take some practice to use them effectively in public places.
So, where are those places of interest? As mentioned earlier, places where many people gather are good places to search. Beaches, riversides, parking lots, parks, outdoor concerts, bus stops, and vending machines are just a few examples. You probably know the best places to search in your area.

There have been reports of people in Manhattan who spend all day searching busy streets for jewelry and other lost items and are able to make a living from it. So start exploring your area and see what treasures you can find!

After all even if the subject here is urban sources of gold, natural gold can be found in traces anywhere even in the middle of a city.

Rivers transport gold from the mountains to the sea. Wherever they pass, there is a chance of finding more or less gold in the black sands of the riverbed.

Old reports on closed mines can be helpful in finding spots that may be interesting.

Using a professional metal detector is more convenient of course. But in some case, that is just not possible. Running around in a city with such a device could arouse suspicion if it is even legal at all.

As usual it is best to keep a low profile and not to cause another modern "Alaska gold rush" in the city we live in.

Try to build a solution, that can work in disguise.

DIY Metal Detector

While you may not have the knowledge today to build this simple and cheap metal detector, you may learn it or know someone who could do it after this instructions. As of today the costs should be around 10 USD - 20 USD. Most parts could also be salvaged from broken elektronics for free. This book should supply you with information for an extreme situation, may it be regonally, globally or personally. In any case, if you have this information available and just need a metal detector, you will be independent from cell services, internet aso. That is the idea. If all that is not the case: Simply buy one!

This DIY metal detector is simple to construct, and can help you find metal objects in the ground. Please note that while this metal detector is functional, it may not be as sensitive or accurate as commercial models.
The tool will help you to detect metal in general. If some finetuning is made or enough experience gained you should even be able to tell whter a pievce of metal iron or gold. But that should not always be expected from these metal detectors.

Materials you will need:

- Arduino (Uno or Nano)
- 10K Ohm resistor
- 100 Ohm resistor
- 10K Ohm potentiometer
- 2N3904 NPN transistor
- 1N4148 diode
- 100µF capacitor
- 0.1µF capacitor
- Buzzer or speaker
- 9V battery and battery clip
- Jumper wires
- Breadboard or wires to connect the pins
- Search coil (you can make this using insulated copper wire, approximately 40-60 turns around a circular frame, like a plastic lid, with a diameter of 6-8 inches)

In case you wire the connctions instead of using a breadboard, you should have a tool like a soldering iron.

Step-by-step guide:

1. Assemble the search coil: Wind the insulated copper wire around a circular frame (plastic lid) 40-60 times, leaving extra wire on both ends for connections. Secure the coil with tape or glue, and ensure it remains flat.
2. Connect the components on the breadboard: Follow these connections:

a. Connect the 10K Ohm resistor between Arduino's 5V output and an empty row on the breadboard.
b. Connect one leg of the 100 Ohm resistor to the same row as the 10K Ohm resistor, and the other leg to an empty row.
c. Connect the 2N3904 transistor's collector to the row with the 100 Ohm resistor, its base to the 10K Ohm resistor, and its emitter to the ground (GND) rail on the breadboard.
d. Connect the 1N4148 diode's anode to the transistor's collector and its cathode to another empty row.
e. Connect one leg of the 0.1μF capacitor to the diode's cathode, and the other leg to the GND rail.
f. Connect one leg of the 100μF capacitor to the diode's cathode, and the other leg to the search coil.
g. Connect the other end of the search coil to the GND rail.
h. Connect the potentiometer's middle pin to Arduino's A0 pin, one outer pin to the 5V output, and the other outer pin to the GND rail.
i. Connect the positive terminal of the buzzer or speaker to Arduino's D2 pin and the negative terminal to the GND rail.
j. Connect the 9V battery to the Arduino using the battery clip.

3. Upload the code: Connect the Arduino to your computer via a USB cable, and upload the following code using the Arduino IDE:

```
const int coilPin = A0;
const int buzzerPin = 2;
int threshold;

void setup() {
  pinMode(coilPin, INPUT);
  pinMode(buzzerPin, OUTPUT);
  Serial.begin(9600);
}

void loop() {
  int coilValue =
analogRead(coilPin);
  threshold = map(analogRead(A1), 0,
1023, 0, 255);

  if (coilValue > threshold) {
    digitalWrite(buzzerPin, HIGH);
    Serial.println("Metal
Detected!");
  } else {
    digitalWrite(buzzerPin, LOW);
  }

  delay(100);
}
```

Test your metal detector: Turn on the Arduino and adjust the potentiometer to set the sensitivity threshold. Start by placing the search coil over a metal object to determine the current sensitivity. If the buzzer does not sound, slowly turn the potentiometer until you reach a point where the buzzer activates when the coil is above a metal object.

4. Fine-tune the sensitivity: Gradually adjust the potentiometer to increase or decrease the sensitivity of the metal detector based on your requirements. Keep in mind that increasing sensitivity might also result in detecting smaller or deeper objects, but it may also produce more false positives.
5. Secure the components: Once you have fine-tuned your metal detector, you can secure the components to a more permanent base, such as a piece of wood or plastic. Ensure that the search coil remains flat, as this will help improve the accuracy of the metal detector.
6. Create a handle: Attach a lightweight rod or PVC pipe to the base where the components are secured, making sure it extends to a comfortable length for you to hold and sweep the search coil over the ground. Attach the Arduino and breadboard to the handle, and make sure all connections remain secure.
7. Waterproof the search coil (optional): If you plan to use your DIY metal detector in wet or damp environments, consider waterproofing the search coil. You can do this by applying a layer of epoxy or a waterproof sealant around the coil, ensuring that the copper wire and connections are protected from moisture.
8. Start treasure hunting: With your DIY metal detector assembled and fine-tuned, you're ready to start searching for precious metals and other valuable objects. Keep in mind that this metal detector is not as accurate or sensitive as commercial models, so you may need to practice and adjust your technique to get the best results.

Low cost DIY metal detectors

In case the preceding DIY metal detector is not within your range of possibilities, there is an even cheaper and more simplified version of such a device. Please note that the performance, however, is far lower, which means it will detect metal only within a very short range. It is a representation of the cheap tools that you find in stores that are intended to detect wires or metal parts in a wall. So, in case you want to secure such a 5 - 10 USD item right now, this is how they look:

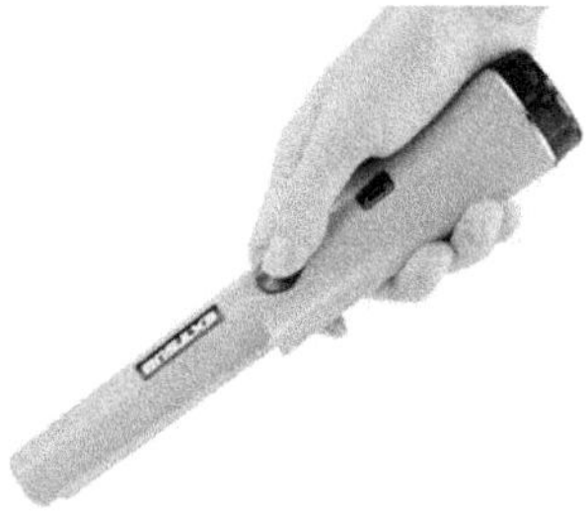

They easily fit into a pocket or a small bag. With a little bit of tuning, they are able to detect metal which is on the surface or a few centimeters below. The author has tried them out in a forest to test their performance, and they can detect objects like coins quite well. Larger objects are even easier to detect. There is a wheel which allows you to adjust the sensitivity. It is really only an improvised solution, but it can be of help one day. If you attach them to a shoe, you could walk around with them without giving away what you are doing.

The item to the left that looks like a flashlight shows a device that is intented for metal detection like in goldhunting. You can also find them a spots where people are searched for weapons. They cost around 30 USD and do a great job. They fit into a backpack or even a larger pocket. They are a great compromise between cost and performance.

They have a very nasty buzzer that indicates a detection. But one could modify it for example and replace it with a vibrating motors like those in a smartphone. Also the red LED lights up if any metal is near.

Ultra low cost DIY metal detector

Here's a simplified version of a metal detector that does not require an Arduino. This metal detector is based on the principle of electromagnetic induction and can detect metallic objects in close proximity, similar to devices used to find electric wires in walls.

Materials you will need:

- 9V battery and battery clip
- 9V battery connector
- Buzzer or speaker
- Insulated copper wire (around 50 feet)
- Cardboard or plastic sheet (to create the search coil)
- Tape or glue (to secure the search coil)
- Small piece of iron or steel (such as a screw or nail)

Step-by-step guide:

- Create the search coil: Cut a cardboard or plastic sheet into a circle with a diameter of about 6 inches. Wind the insulated copper wire around the circular frame 40-50 times, leaving extra wire on both ends for connections. Secure the coil with tape or glue, and ensure it remains flat.
- Attach the battery connector: Connect the 9V battery clip to the 9V battery connector, making sure the red (positive) wire is connected to the positive terminal of the connector and the black (negative) wire is connected to the negative terminal.
- Connect the buzzer or speaker: Connect the positive (red) wire of the battery connector to the positive terminal of the buzzer or speaker, and the negative (black) wire to the negative terminal.
- Attach the iron or steel piece: Tape or glue a small piece of iron or steel (such as a screw or nail) to the buzzer or speaker, ensuring it is in contact with the metal casing.
- Connect the search coil: Connect one end of the search coil wire to the metal casing of the buzzer or speaker, and the other end to the piece of iron or steel.

Test the metal detector:

Connect the battery to the battery clip, and hold the search coil close to a metallic object. The buzzer or speaker should produce a sound when in close proximity to the metal. If the sound is too faint, adjust the position of the iron or steel piece on the buzzer or speaker to increase the sensitivity.

Please note that this simplified metal detector has limited range and sensitivity compared to an Arduino-based or commercial model. It is suitable for detecting metal objects in close proximity, such as wires in walls or small metallic objects.

DIY Precious Metal Tester

These instructions will help you build a DIY device that distinguishes between Precious Metals and Base Metals.

Step 1: Prepare a glass or spraybottle with **clean** distilled water.

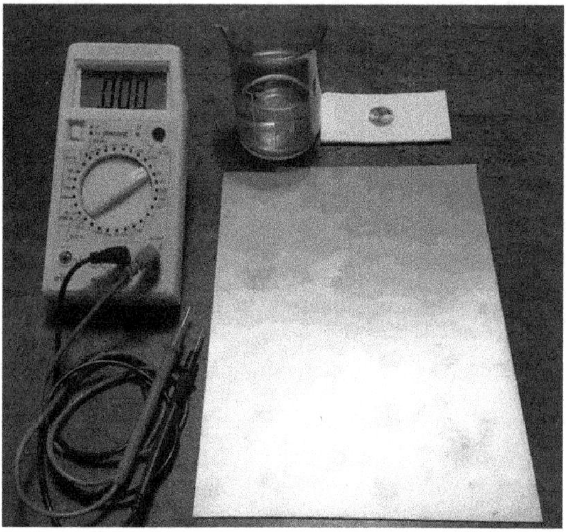

Step 2: Take a small flat sheet of copper, preferably pure 999 Copper. Clean it with alcohol to remove any grease or glue, then rinse with distilled water. Avoid using aggressive chemicals like acid or alkaline cleaners.

Step 3: Use a clean white cotton cloth, or a clean tissue or cloth of any color. Avoid any cloth with grease, metal chips, or dust. Place the cloth on the Copper sheet or object, leaving a small area or corner uncovered.

Step 5: Wet the cloth with the prepared solution. Do not

wet the uncovered area. The cloth should be wet but not swimming in water. Just so that it is wet and water is not dripping from the cloth, or at least not much.

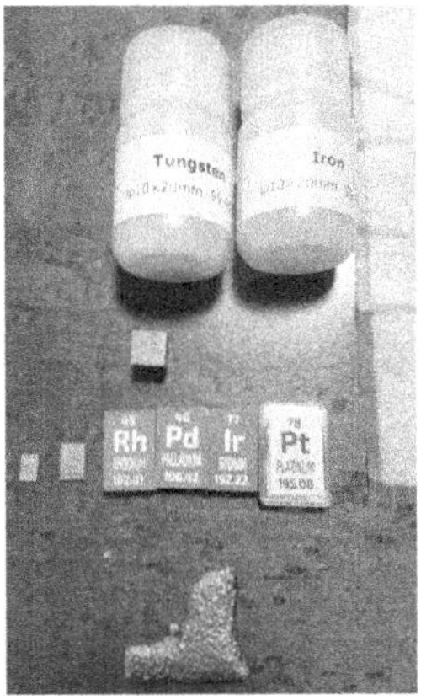

Step 6: Put another piece of Copper on top of the cloth, preferably known pure Copper. It can be Copper-plated as well, so most cent coins are plated in more or less pure Copper. For our purpose, they will do the job.

Step 7: Use a multimeter and set the voltage type to "DC." Set the range of the multimeter to 2V if possible or below, down to 1 or 1000mV. Connect the - probe (usually black, often labeled "Ground") to the uncovered, dry corner of the copper sheet or copper object beneath the cloth, and the other probe (usually red) to the copper object on top of the cloth. Your multimeter, whether digital or analog, should react a little bit for a short moment, then remain at around 0V, let´s say -30 mV to +30 mV. If there is a calibration button on your multimeter, use it to set it to zero.

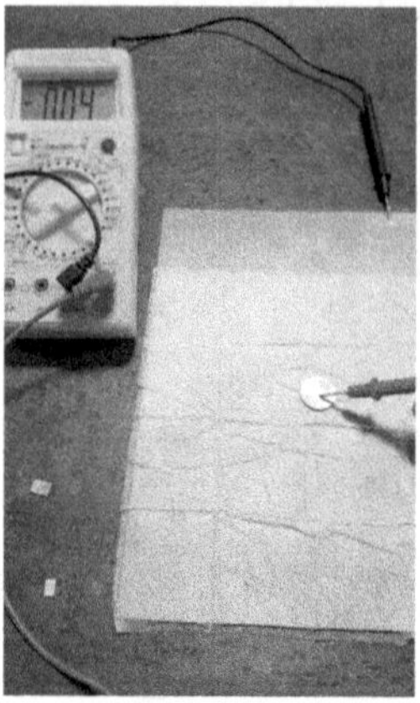 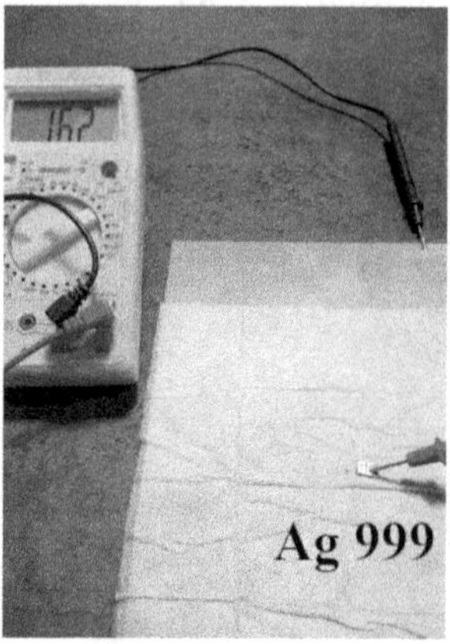

Step 8: Take the object that you want to test and put it on top of the (still wet!) cloth. Repeat Step 7 in the same way: the black -probe to the clean dry edge of the Copper underneath and the + or red probe to the object you want to test. You can use scotch tape to attach the probe to the Copper sheet. That way one hand remains free.

If your multimeter reads above 50mV, around 100mV, it indicates a Precious Metal. A negative voltage, such as -100mV, suggests a base metal. Below: 999 Gold and molten e-waste from Palladium and Silver loaded MLCC capacitors.

Note that this method only detects metals on the surface of an object. Gold-plated items may show up as Precious Metals even if the core is cheap Base Metal, while a molten metal with 5% Platinum may be detected as Base Metal. This DIY method is useful for detecting Precious Metals if they are present in a considerable amount or as plating on the surface, but it's not comprehensive for all metal detection questions.

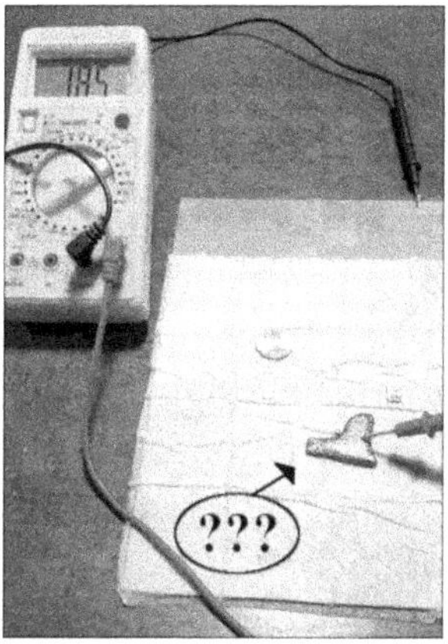

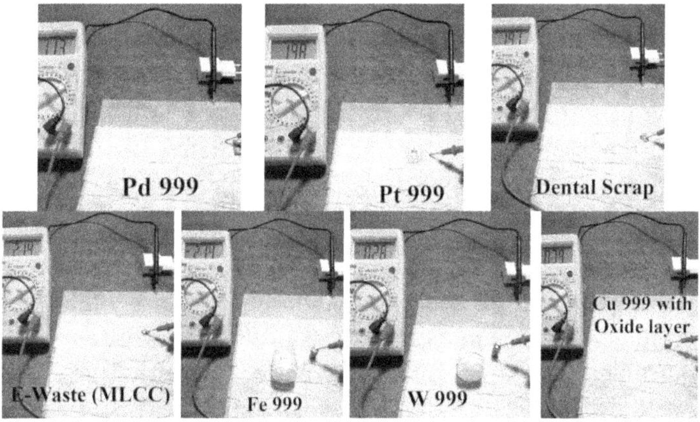

Some more test results

To ensure accurate results, keep the cloth damp but not too wet. A dry cloth will not work correctly and may lead to confusing results. Change the cloth after each test to avoid contamination from base metals. Temperature and humidity can affect the results, so perform the test at room temperature for the best outcome. This method is a quick, non-destructive tool suitable for testing jewelry and other items without the need for a scratch or acid test, although results may not always be accurate.

Note that your results may vary depending on so many factors that it makes no sense to try to compensate them in such a low cost solution. It is only important to check for the polarity of the result or how close it is to 0 V. Note that the Precious Metals always have a possitive voltage reading whereas the base Metals return a negative voltage.

Perform a calibration run before testing using copper and a well-known Precious Metal like Fine Gold to ensure probes are in order. Note the results and compare with known samples when testing an unknown object to determine the metal type. Replace the cloth frequently for conclusive and repeatable results since the setup's chemical composition changes with each test.

Note that the results may vary depending on how the probe contacts the metal, especially for alloys or molten samples. This test cannot provide quantitative statements or determine the ratio of metals in the sample.

The BozzTech MTI00X Metal Tester is based on this Redox principle. It compensates for these variables, and it offers a more convenient and repeatable assessment by displaying results in graphical format on a PC screen, using AI technology among other benefits.

Refining scrap gold

Recovering ends and refining starts when dissolving gold with chemicals.

If you decide to refine gold, either your own collected or raw material that has been bought from others, be aware that it takes some time and skill, and you will have to go through a phase of experience where some things will go wrong.

Always perform chemical reactions outside or in an area where the fumes can cause no harm. Even with the best preparation, there will be fumes, and they are harmful to your health, the environment, and the people around you.

The procedures in this book are not so in-depth that they can be reproduced without a basic knowledge of chemistry. Therefore, understanding the fundamentals should be the first step before buying any chemicals or even performing any refining procedures. Refining is often not needed to sell scrap gold. It may be helpful in achieving higher prices and making the material easier to sell (not every gold buyer will buy unfinished material), but that is always up to the situation. A 14K gold button is not pure, but still 14K. If the gold is estimated to be below 14K, refining should be considered.

Apart from the health risks and the additional costs for refining, there is also a serious risk of losing money, especially for the beginner. When dissolving gold and precipitating it again, many things can go wrong, and often the gold stays lost in the netherworld or is poured into the sink without knowing it.

Sometimes when dissolving gold, not all of it is dissolved. The undissolved gold sometimes remains undetected, especially if it is inside objects such as microchips, etc. Using the right amount of nitric acid in Aqua Regia is complicated. Many beginners use too much and then have problems precipitating the gold back. The solution stays too “strong” and won't give the gold back anymore.

It all sounds very simple when reading the instructions on how to use Aqua Regia and other chemicals, but one must not forget that each batch of material is different in composition and some other factors, and surprises can happen at any time.

All in all, a “dirty” gold button is still better than none. Refining for the small-scale gold scrapper should only be done if there is no other way.

Tools and chemicals

Listed below are some basic tools and chemicals for refining precious metals.

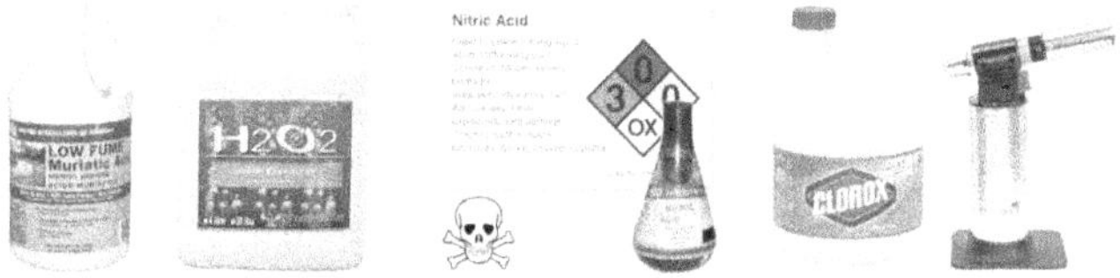

Hydrochloric acid; Chemical name: hydrochloric acid or **HCl**. Can be bought as cement cleaner (concentration 25%) in most larger stores in the homeworking department.

Hydrogen Peroxide; Chemical name **H_2O_2**.

H_2O_2 comes in many shapes, bottles, plastic tanks and concentrations. 7% -12% will do. Make sure that there is as little additive, like silver or aluminum, as possible.

Nitric acid; Chemical symbol: **HNO_3**.

Avoid the usage whenever you can.

Don´t breath the brown fumes. Never use indoors!

Chlorox/Chlorix also Dan Klorix or similar bleach. Do not confuse with the drug Chlorex which is used to treat cold. Choose a product without or only minimal additive, such as perfume, color, metal powder etc.

Blow torch Must have a butane-propane mix gas to achieve 1200°C for melting gold.

About hydrochloric acid

Hydrochloric acid, also known as muriatic acid or HCl, is a medium-strength acid often used to extract precious metals from materials. Hydrochloric acid dissolves base metals like iron and nickel but does not affect gold.

Another application of hydrochloric acid is creating a test solution to detect precious metals such as gold, palladium, and platinum. This test solution is made by mixing hydrochloric acid with pure tin to create stannous chloride.

Hydrochloric acid can also be used to dissolve gold, usually in a mix with nitric acid called aqua regia. However, nitric acid is difficult to obtain and sometimes even prohibited in certain countries. In this case, an alternative method involves mixing hydrochloric acid with Chlorex or a similar drain cleaner to dissolve gold. This process must be done outside due to the extremely noxious and harmful fumes produced.

For urban gold miners, hydrochloric acid is one of the most useful chemicals. If hydrochloric acid is not available, organic acids like citric acid or vinegar can be used to dissolve base metals, though it may require more time and heat.

About H_2O_2

H_2O_2 or Hydrogen Peroxide is used in many ways without consumers even knowing it. 3% H_2O_2 is used as a teeth whitener and can be bought at most pharmacies. 7%-12% H_2O_2 is used for bleaching hair and can be found in hair salons or in pharmacies and drugstores.

There are chemicals used for creating oxygen in a fish tank, which also create H_2O_2, but the other reaction products create a caustic solution, so this is not useful for our purposes in refining.

How to make a simple electrolytic cell

A very basic electrolytic cell only needs 3 basic components:

- a vessel in which water is being put.
- a source of DC energy like a car battery or a battery charger with cables and clamps.
- and finally the material that the electrolytic cell should process.

This material can either be gold plated or silver plated material.
The function of the electrolytic cell is to deplate this precious metal from a base metal. Those cells are very popular for deplating silver cutlery or silver plated contacts.
Using normal tap water = H_2O as electrolyte makes this process very easy and safe but also very slow and not so effective.

Important! This process works with DC power only ! Do not try to use AC power especially not the one from your wall outlet!

The AC voltage of this outlet in combination with water can kill you!

This process is a low voltage, low power process ! Don´t experiment with other power sources than those described!

A small amount of acid should be added to increase the electronic conductivity of the electrolyte. It doesn't have to be a powerful and dangerous acid; a few spoons of citric acid or vinegar will suffice. Even salt can help to improve the speed of the process. However, some users may not have access to any acid, so they could still add some salt to the water, or they may prefer to use pure water for the process.

Here's how it works:
Set up a vessel, preferably transparent, and fill it with water.
Take a piece of lead and sink it into the vessel. Connect it to the Minus pole of your car battery, battery charger, or PC power supply. This will be your cathode from now on.
On the opposite side of the vessel, dip in the object that you want to deplate (such as a silver-plated spoon).

Connect it to the PLUS pole of your power source. Depending on your setup, the deplating of the silver will take minutes or hours, and if no acid is used, even days.

A white cloud will form underneath the object and create a white layer on the bottom of the vessel. This is silver and silver oxide.

Once the object has been completely deplated, it has to be removed to avoid the underlying base metals from dissolving, so the electrolytic cell is a process that requires attention.

Making your own nitric acid

Since the regulation of chemicals has increased in the past years, it has become difficult for many small refiners to obtain important chemicals in many countries, especially nitric acid, which is often hard to get. If needed, there is a way to produce nitric acid out of nothing more than thin air. The air that we breathe and that surrounds us consists of nearly 80% nitrogen. We can make use of that and extract it in a simple but very slow and ineffective DIY process. However, that may be better than nothing.

Do some research on the DIY Birkeland-Eyde Reactor. The setup is simple, using a special transformer, some glassware, and pipes. If you want to learn more about this possibility, check out this great video on YouTube made by the channel DBX labs, formerly known as Cody's Lab.
https://www.youtube.com/watch?v=4spP-L-RuGY

About Cyanide and Mercury and Aqua Regia

As a father and a responsible individual, I have been hesitant to share some of the "dark corners" of metal refining. It would be a nightmare for me if someone got injured or suffered any damage from incorrectly using the information provided here. I have contemplated this matter for a long time, and after seeing numerous tragic reports about children trying to make a living from gold scrapping or uneducated people unknowingly harming themselves or others with dangerous techniques, I decided to provide additional information on these topics. This information is intended to help you understand the risks you're dealing with, and if you find yourself in an extreme situation, you'll know the dangers involved and why. If possible, avoid using these substances, as you will put yourself in great danger if something goes wrong!

We'll start with the least dangerous method, but still dangerous! The most dangerous will be described last.

Aqua Regia

Aqua Regia is a mixture of hydrochloric acid (also called muriatic acid, technically HCl) and nitric acid (technically called HNO3).

Why is it being used?

Aqua Regia can dissolve gold. No other single acid can

do that. It is very easy to obtain.

What are the dangers?
While Aqua Regia dissolves gold and other metals, a dark orange-brown fume is emitted. This fume is primarily composed of so-called NOx gases which can destroy lung cells if inhaled and cause severe diseases, such as impotence in men or harm to unborn children in pregnant women. The effects on the lungs can be observed and noticed within hours. Some damage might be irreversible. That is why one should never perform Aqua Regia inside a closed room. If necessary, a ventilated fume hood should be used to transport the fumes outside. The fumes are very corrosive, so the fume hood and the ventilator will break down quickly if they contain any metal. Generally, Aqua Regia is used outdoors, which is better but not perfect because the user can still inhale the dangerous fumes. A simple mask will not be sufficient. Bystanders, family members, etc., nearby are also at risk.

Using Aqua Regia exposes you to a very high long-term health risk to your lungs, organs, and unborn children. It exposes you to an immediate risk to your lungs if you inhale the fumes.

Mercury

Mercury is a metal that is liquid at room temperture. Looks shiny, forms small spheres, that will roll over a surface like little balls. It used to be very common in analoqe thermometrs, but due to it´s toxity it has been replaced with Gallium, another liquid metal, if not by digital thermometers. Mercury is not rare in nature. It is difficult to obtain, due to regulations in most countries, but in fact mercury is presnt in many items (such as low energy bulbs, battery cells (Read the chapter about the batteries on that) and other items. So if needed it still can be found an concentrated to a higher level.

Why is it being used?

Mercury can incapsulate gold. If gold is present in the form of very fine powder, mercury will wrap itself around it and therefore seperate the gold from the non-gold particles. No other chemical can do that.

How is it being used?

There are two common methods for using mercury to extract gold from raw material.
As described above, sand containing fine gold powder is brought into contact with mercury. Typically, a gold pan is used for this process. Water is added, and the mercury wraps itself around the tiny gold particles. The pan is agitated to ensure as much gold as possible is captured inside the mercury hull. All water-soluble material is washed away with the water in the swirling gold pan. The non-water-soluble components of the material are selected by hand or shoveled over the edge of the pan. In the final stage, one large mercury bubble forms with all the fine gold particles trapped inside.
This compound is then transferred to another beaker or vessel and - the most dangerous part - heated so that the mercury evaporates, leaving the pure gold behind.
Mercury is also used to cover gold-loaded material such

as sand.

Below is an illustration of industrial equipment and the steps of mercury extraction. These images have been provided by the Chinese company Jiangxi Hengchang Mining Machinery Manufacturing Co., Ltd.

Note from the author:

I have no affiliation with them or any financial benefit, it is just free advertising for them. So if you buy such a machine and make a fortune, it would be nice if you invite me for a dinner or so ;-)

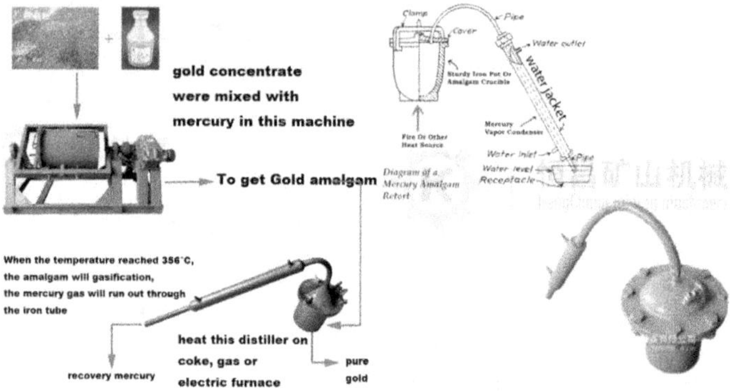

This illustration is useful because it shows the entire process and how you could improvise a safer way of using mercury. It is crucial to have a pipe on the vessel containing the mercury-gold mix, called amalgam, so the toxic mercury can condense safely without leaving the process chamber and be collected in the water.

Another very primitive method, often used by micro-scale miners in developing countries, doesn't incorporate any tools at all but instead uses a cloth like a t-shirt or something similar. The user mixes mercury with raw material consisting of fine gold powder and non-gold material. The mercury forms an amalgam, just like before. Then, this amalgam, which is a liquid bubble that encapsulates the gold, is placed into a piece of cloth. A bowl or pan is positioned underneath the cloth. The cloth is then pressed. Due to the force applied, the mercury separates from the gold and passes through the cloth's fibers. Once done, the pure gold remains in the cloth, while the mercury has dripped into a prepared vessel and can be reused.

What are the dangers?

Mercury has a low boiling point, slightly above room temperature. If it boils and is inhaled, it can cause severe damage to your brain. Mercury can penetrate the skin barrier, so working with it without protection like gloves may lead to absorption, with the mercury potentially remaining in your body forever. This effect is known as "Mercury fever."

Mercury can cause significant brain damage and harm unborn children. The effects are not immediate but develop over days, weeks, or sometimes months. As a metal, even liquid at room temperature, mercury doesn't mix with pure water, so it's safe to store under water. However, mercury forms compounds with other metals or chemicals found in nature. Releasing mercury into natural water reservoirs allows it to combine with other substances in lakes or rivers, making removal practically impossible. Mercury ends up in the food chain, affecting fish and other animals humans consume, ultimately causing devastating effects. This long-term danger spans years and decades.

The short to mid-term danger is inhaling mercury, as its low vaporization point allows it to evaporate on a sunny day. Skin contamination with mercury also puts a person at significant risk of "Mercury fever," leading to impaired perception, brain malfunction, and potentially lifelong brain damage. Unborn children may suffer irreversible bodily and brain damage. A person might never rid their body of the mercury, which can even remain in their corpse after death.

Where to get mercury from in extreme situations

Mercury can accumulate in both plants and animal-based foods, especially fish and shellfish. It's important to note that the mercury levels in these foods may vary depending on the level of pollution in the environment where they are sourced. Some examples of fish and shellfish with higher mercury levels include:

- Swordfish
- Shark
- King mackerel
- Tilefish (Gulf of Mexico)

While most plants do not typically accumulate high

levels of mercury, certain plants can absorb mercury from polluted soil or water sources. The amount of mercury in these plants will vary depending on the level of contamination in their environment. Some examples include:

- Water hyacinth
- Duckweed
- Indian mustard
- Sunflower

Remember that mercury is a metal, but it also has a low vaporization point. So, burning these natural sources will cause mercury to evaporate, not accumulate. This book provides only basic information. To extract a significant amount of mercury from these fishes or plants, you would need a large quantity. Moreover, the amount of mercury in these materials highly depends on how much they absorbed during their lifetime. However, it is still possible, because they are natural mercury accumulators. To extract the mercury, the material needs to be decayed, composted, or concentrated in some other way. Also, remember that mercury will not mix with pure water.

Mercury forms an amalgam with gold, attracting fine gold powder and changing its surface to silver when in contact with even tiny amounts of mercury. This could potentially concentrate mercury in the setting. However, this method is untested and may require a significant amount of organic material, making it suitable only for extreme situations.

Cyanides for extracting gold

Why is it being used?

Cyanide compounds have the unique feature of dissolving gold selectively. No other common substance is able to do that

How is it being used?

Upon contact with a gold covered or purely golden object, cyanides will leach gold and put it into a suspension. From there the almsot pure gold can be precipated.

What are the dangers?

The danger of working with cyanides is instant death, if used the wrong way.

The promise sounds like magic: Cyanid compounds that are solid and appear like tablesalt, are often highly water soluable. Just put some of the powder in water and you will get a solution that will leach gold from any surface within seconds.
Cynids are the holy grail of gold recovery, but they are also Pandorras box.
In solid form cynid compounds are very stable, do not react much with other reagents and therefore pose no imminent threat. It is even so, that cynod compound are a part of our food, wheter it was grown naturally or industrial produced one. One should not digest, breath

in oder get in touch with them, like with any other chemical named here. But they remain relatively "harmless" opposed to caids, mercury and so on.

So even though they can be found in everyday items like ordinary tablesalt (check the ingriedients fpr cyanide), they are strongly regulated and practically impossible to obtain for private purposes in concentrated form

There is one special condition that is ultimately dangerous: If cyanid compounds get into contact with acids!

If that is the case they omit vapours that are deadly with less than a minute if inhaled.

This has been used f.e. in the "Third Reich" for massmurder purposes.

So don´t get fooled by the appaerance of cyanid compounds in everyday items. The "sleep" and rest inactive as long as they do not get "awoken" by mixing the wrong chemicals into the solution. There are many types of acids and sometimes it is not even clear that and acid is being used or formed while performing recovery.

One wrong mislabeled bottel that contains an acid one short breath and you are dead.

Don´t use them unless you are an expert and di have the professional epuipment, skills and knowledge. It is never worth it.

Making your own cyanides

This book addresses users in very delicate, extreme situations. I will now provide some starting points on how to produce cyanide compounds in extreme scenarios when no other options are available. Ensure you gather as much information about cyanide compounds before starting the production process. Always remember that solid cyanide compounds are relatively safe to handle but should never be ingested or touched with bare hands. Most importantly, avoid contact with any acids once the concentration process begins. This method may be highly inefficient and absolutely uneconomical, but it is a possible approach in truly dire circumstances. This is by no means a standard procedure!

Cyanide compounds can be found in many plants.
Here are approximate numbers for the cyanide content in some natural sources:

- Cassava (yuca or manioc) - Cyanide content varies between 15-400 mg/kg in the roots and up to 3,000 mg/kg in the leaves, depending on the variety.
- Apricot kernels - Bitter apricot kernels can contain between 0.5-3.5 mg of hydrogen cyanide per gram, while sweet apricot kernels contain significantly less.Lima beans - These beans contain 20-30 mg of cyanide per 100 grams of dry weight.
- Apple seeds - The cyanide content is estimated to be around 1-4 mg of hydrogen cyanide per gram of apple seeds.
- Bamboo shoots - Raw bamboo shoots can contain up to 1,000 mg of cyanide per kg, depending on the species.

The cyanide content in these sources can vary based on factors like plant variety, growing conditions, and preparation methods.

- Extracting cyanide compounds from natural sources should be done with extreme caution, as these compounds are highly toxic. It is not recommended to attempt this process without proper training and safety measures. However, if you must do so, you may consider the following general steps:
- Choose a natural source with a high cyanide content, such as cassava, apricot kernels, or lima beans.
- Crush or grind the material to release the cyanide compounds. It is essential to wear personal protective equipment (PPE), including gloves, goggles, and a mask or respirator, to avoid exposure to the cyanide.Create an alkaline solution by dissolving a base, like sodium hydroxide, in water. Alkaline conditions help release cyanide as the soluble cyanide salt.
- Mix the crushed material with the alkaline solution and stir well. This step should be done in a well-ventilated area or under a fume hood to prevent inhalation of toxic gases.
- Allow the mixture to settle, and then filter or decant the liquid, which contains the dissolved cyanide compounds.

- You can precipitate the cyanide compounds by adding an acid, such as hydrochloric acid, until the pH reaches around 4. (Read on to learn how to improvie a PH meter)The cyanide will form a solid precipitate, which can be collected by filtration.
- Wash and dry the precipitate to remove impurities. Store the cyanide compound in a well-labeled, sealed container, away from heat sources and out of reach of children and pets.

Please note that this is a general outline, and the actual extraction process may vary depending on the specific natural source and cyanide compounds present. It is crucial to research and follow proper safety protocols and procedures to minimize the risks associated with handling cyanide.

Improvised pH meter

When working with cyanides it is extremly important to be in control of the PH value of your solution. It is vital! If you lose control, the solution can become a deadly threat to you by omitting gases that wil kill you within seconds!

pH is a scale used to measure the acidity or alkalinity of a solution. It ranges from 0 to 14. A pH of 7 is considered neutral, meaning it is neither acidic nor alkaline.

Solutions with a pH value below 7 are acidic, while those with a pH value above 7 are alkaline (also called basic). The lower the pH value, the stronger the acid; the higher the pH value, the stronger the base.

In simple terms, pH tells us if a solution is acidic, alkaline, or neutral.

In an acidic environment (pH below 9), cyanide can convert into a toxic gas called hydrogen cyanide. Hydrogen cyanide is dangerous because it can be inhaled, leading to serious health risks. To minimize the risk of hydrogen cyanide gas formation, it is important to maintain a pH above 9 when working with cyanide solutions. Creating a makeshift pH meter using simple means can be done with the red cabbage pH indicator I previously mentioned. This method will not be very precise, but it's better than having no pH testing at all. If possible, consider using commercial pH test kits, like the ones available for swimming pools or aquariums.

Remember, This can make the difference for you between life and death!

Here's how to make a red cabbage pH indicator:

Chop up a small portion of red cabbage.

Boil the cabbage in water for about 10-15 minutes. The water will turn purple due to the anthocyanin.

Let the water cool down and then strain it to separate the cabbage from the colored water. The purple liquid is your pH indicator.

Now, you can use this red cabbage pH indicator to test the pH of different solutions. The color changes are approximate:

pH 8 and above: The indicator turns shades of green, which means the solution is alkaline (or basic).

pH 7 to 8: The indicator turns blue or blue-green, indicating that the solution is near-neutral or slightly basic.

pH 7: The indicator remains purple, which indicates a neutral solution.

pH below 7: The indicator turns shades of pink or red, indicating that the solution is acidic.

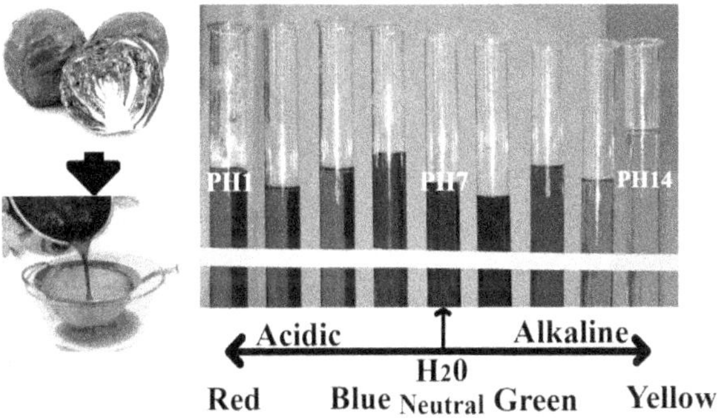

Please note that the color changes may not be exact, and this DIY pH indicator is best used for a rough estimation of pH levels.

Converting units

If you read more literature on gold scrapping, you may come across many expressions and units that are unfamiliar to you. Especially when working with chemicals, it is crucial to understand the units in which any recipe was intended. Please note that different countries have different decimal notations. In standard SI units, a "," represents the decimal point and a "." is used as a separator for each multiple of thousands. For instance, a value of one thousand euros and ten cents would be written as 1.000,10 €. If you encounter non-metric values, please ensure that you understand the notation of the comma (",") and the dot (".") to ensure that you have interpreted the values correctly.

Length

Inch vs mm vs inch

Inch	mm
1	25.4
2	50.8
3	76.19
5	127
10	254
25	635
50	1270
100	2540
200	5080
1000	2540

mm	Inch
1	0.03937
2	0.07874
3	0.11811
5	0.19685
10	0.39370
25	0.98425
50	1.96850
100	3.93700
200	7.87400
1000 =1m	39.37000

Calculation:

where A = value in inch, B= value in mm

A = B x 25,4   B = A x 0,03937

Weight

Lbs vs kg

Pounds (lbs)	Kilo-gram (kg)	Note
¼ or 0,25	0.113	
1/3 or 0,33	0.150	
½ or 0,5	0.227	
¾ or 0,75	0.340	
1	0.454	
2	0.907	
5	2.268	
10	4.536	
20	9.072	
50	22.680	
100	45.359	
200	90.718	

Ounce vs g & Troy ounce vs g

Ounce vs g

Ounce (Oz)	Gram (g)	Note
½ or 0.5	14.18	
1	28.35	
2	56.7	
3	85.05	
5	141.75	

Troy ounce vs g

Troy ounce (oz.tr)	Gram (g)	Note
½ or 0.5	15.5517	
1	31.1035	Gold price basis
2	62.2070	
3	93.3104	
5	155.5174	

Important: There are 2 different ounce standards in the anglo-american system. Troy ounce is being used for precious metals only, whereby ounce can be used for anything. The gold price is based on the troy ounce.

Volume of liquids

US gallon vs liter

Gallon	Liter (l)	Note
1	3.79	One good bucket full
2	7.57	
3	11.36	
5	18.93	
10	37.9	

Calculating gold plating

Surface of the plating

Often gold plated pins are found in electronics. To calculate their content of gold they should be considered as an ideal cylinder.

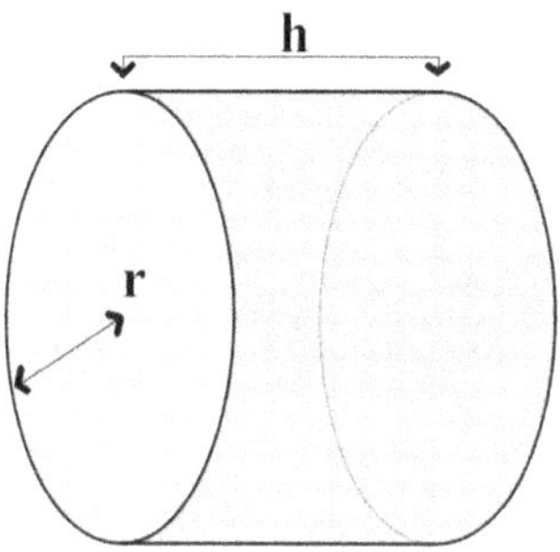

The surface area of such an object is:

$$A = 2\pi r^2 + 2\pi rh = 2\pi r(r + h)$$

whereby:

r = radius =1/2 diameter

h = height or length of pin

π = (say:"pi") = 3,14159

If the pin is not completely even in regards to its diameter, average size is good enough.

Volume of the plating

To calculate the volume of the plating the surface is

multiplied with the thickness of the plating.
In many cases this thickness is unknown. The typical plating for electronic contacts can vary from 0,1 micron to 5 micron (4 – 200 micro inch).
Some typical plating with applications

Type	Thickness	Application
Flash gold	0,05-0,3 micron	Low cost contacts & coatings
Pure gold	0,5-2,5 micron	High end electronics
Hart gold	0,1-2 micron	Electrical contacts
	8/16 micron	"Goldfinger" from PC cards

1 micron stands for $1\times10-^{6}$ m = 1 millionth of a meter.
US units:
1 micron equals 3.2808×10^{-6} ft or $39{,}370\times10^{-6}$ in
So the volume of a gold plating of a pin/cylinder is:

$$\mathbf{V = A \times h_t}$$

Where h_t is the thickness of the plating.

Mass of the plating

Now with the given volume of the plating and the known Density ρ (say: "Rho") of pure gold which is 19,32 g/cm^3 the total mass of the gold that is plated onto the pin can be calculated. As follows:

$$\mathbf{m = v \times \rho}$$

or

mass = volume multiplied with density

When making these calculations, remember that all numbers involved are very small, down to the millionth of a meter and so it is advisable to use the scientific mode of the calculator and use $1\times10{-}6$ instead of 0.000001, which may cause errors due to rounding.

In these calculations, we assume that the plated gold is 24 carats or 999.99 gold. Otherwise, the lower gold purity and its factor have to be taken into account. If the gold is only 8 carats, then the final result has to be divided by three since 24 is equal to 3 multiplied by 8.

As a result, you now have the mass of gold plated on one single pin or other cylindrical object. This value now has to be multiplied by the number of pins in the batch to determine the total amount of gold in it.

Temperature units

Listed below are three different temperature units and their respective values, plus certain important temperature points.
Although degree Celsius is the official international unit for temperatures today, Fahrenheit is still often found in US literature, especially when it was printed before the year 2000. Kelvin is usually used in scientific literature.

Celsius	Fahren-heit	Kelvin	Note
-20	-4	253.15	
-15	5	258.15	
-10	14	263.15	
-5	23	268.15	
-2	28.4	271.15	
0	32	273.15	Pure water freezes
4	39.2	277.15	
5	41	278.15	
10	50	283.15	
15	59	288.15	
20	68	293.15	Room temperature
25	77	298.15	
30	86	303.15	
35	95	308.15	

Celsius	Fahren-heit	Kelvin	Note
40	104	313.15	
45	113	318.15	
50	122	323.15	
55	131	328.15	
60	140	333.15	
65	149	338.15	
70	158	343.15	
80	167	353.15	
85	185	358.15	
90	194	363.15	
100	203	373.15	Boiling point of water
150	302	423.15	
200	392	473.15	
232	450	505.15	Melting point Tin
400	752	673.15	
600	1112	873.15	
800	1472	1073.15	
900	1652	1173.15	
962	1764	1235.15	Melting point Silver
1000	1832	1273.15	
1060	1940	1333.15	Melting point Gold
1084	1983	1357.15	Melting point Copper
1200	2192	1473.15	
1400	2552	1673.15	
1500	2732	1773.15	
1555	2831	1828.15	Melting point Palladium

Purity of gold

Gold purity varies globally, with 99.999% considered 100%. The EU forbids calling "Gold 333" an alloy, as it contains 33% gold by mass but only 15%-20% by volume considering atom weights. Gold 333 lacks gold's known properties, so the minimum purity grade called "gold" is now 375. Carat 7 and below are uncommon for jewelry. Diamond "carat" is unrelated to gold purity "carat" or "karat."

Carat	Tradename	Note	Purity (%)	Carat
24	Gold 999 Fine gold Feingold Pure gold Chuk Kam	Even pure gold always shows minimal traces of other metals. Popular in Far East (China Hong Kong, Taiwan) Malaysia, Indonesia	100	24
23			95.83	23
22	Gold 916	Arabic countries, Southafrica (Bullion), Bangladesch, India, Pakistan and Sri Lanka, UK	91.67	22
21.6			90	21.6
21	Gold 875	Arabic countries, Gulf Region	87.5	21
20			83.33	20
19.2		Southern Europe, Portugal	80	19.2
19			79.17	19
18	Gold 750	USA, Southern Europe, Egypt, Germany	75	18
17			70.83	17
16			66.67	16
15			62.5	15
14	Gold 585	USA, Germany, Russia	58.33	14
13			54.17	13
12			50	12
11			45.83	11
10		USA	41.67	10
9	Gold 375	Minmum in EU for gold, Russia,UK	37.5	9
8	Gold 333	Old minimal standard Germany	33.33	8
7			29.17	7
6			25	6
5			20.83	5
4			16.67	4
3			12.5	3
2			8.33	2
1			4.17	1

Periodic System

Group → / ↓ Period	1	2	3	4	5	6	7	8	9	10	11	12	13	14	15	16	17	18
1	1 H																	2 He
2	3 Li	4 Be											5 B	6 C	7 N	8 O	9 F	10 Ne
3	11 Na	12 Mg											13 Al	14 Si	15 P	16 S	17 Cl	18 Ar
4	19 K	20 Ca	21 Sc	22 Ti	23 V	24 Cr	25 Mn	26 Fe	27 Co	28 Ni	29 Cu	30 Zn	31 Ga	32 Ge	33 As	34 Se	35 Br	36 Kr
5	37 Rb	38 Sr	39 Y	40 Zr	41 Nb	42 Mo	43 Tc	44 Ru	45 Rh	46 Pd	47 Ag	48 Cd	49 In	50 Sn	51 Sb	52 Te	53 I	54 Xe
6	55 Cs	56 Ba		72 Hf	73 Ta	74 W	75 Re	76 Os	77 Ir	78 Pt	79 Au	80 Hg	81 Tl	82 Pb	83 Bi	84 Po	85 At	86 Rn
7	87 Fr	88 Ra		104 Rf	105 Db	106 Sg	107 Bh	108 Hs	109 Mt	110 Ds	111 Rg	112 Cn	113 Uut	114 Uuq	115 Uup	116 Uuh	117 Uus	118 Uuo
Lanthanides				57 La	58 Ce	59 Pr	60 Nd	61 Pm	62 Sm	63 Eu	64 Gd	65 Tb	66 Dy	67 Ho	68 Er	69 Tm	70 Yb	71 Lu
Actinides				89 Ac	90 Th	91 Pa	92 U	93 Np	94 Pu	95 Am	96 Cm	97 Bk	98 Cf	99 Es	100 Fm	101 Md	102 No	103 Lr

Translating special terms

In semi-professional literature or on the internet, you may come across expressions or chemical names that are uncommon. When working with chemicals, it is crucial to know their scientific name and meaning.

Bleach = H_2O_2 or NaClO

This means a strong oxidizer. It can be H_2O_2 (peroxide-based) or chlorine-based, like NaClO (sodium hypochlorite), which is a very popular household bleach product.

GF, gf or gold-filled = A special, thick gold plating.

HCL+CL; CL=NaClO = The CL stands for chlorine based bleach. (Chlorex/ Chlorix/ Dan Klorix) etc)

Lye = NaOH/KOH

General term for strong alkali. Usually meaning sodium hydroxide or potassium hydroxide

Potassium = K

Another term for periodic element 19 = K = Kalium

SMB = Sodium Metabisulfite = $Na_2S_2O_5$

Selectively precipitates gold from goldchloride solution

Useful links

Youtube channel on recovering and refining

The video channel of this author
http://goo.gl/xf8tE

Sam´s channel (Gold´n scrap)
http://goo.gl/0gAaG

Forum, Websites and stores on Gold recovery

Goldrefining Forum - the best, worldwide!
http://goo.gl/gzl6I

Lazersteve´s store - many interesting items for refiner.
http://goo.gl/ORkya

Partnor´s ebay store (chemicals and supplies)
http://goo.gl/VuwJy

Please tell them, that you found their shops though this book, maybe there will be a special offer for you.

Note: Links have been shortened for your convenience.

Final conclusions

This handbook provides a compact and basic overview of today's urban mining. However, there is much more to learn and discover. If you are interested in this subject and need additional information, the internet is a good place to start.

There are many different types of precious metal scrap and recovery procedures, and no single book can display them all. Once you have decided which kind of scrap you want to pursue, it is time to seek more specialized and in-depth information.

This handbook is priced economically so that anyone can afford it. If I have piqued your interest in urban mining and gold scrapping and you would like to delve into further details, check out the extended edition of this title.

If you find the book helpful, I would appreciate a good rating on Amazon. Thank you!

If you find this book useful and have obtained it as an e-book or another digital form, consider buying the printed version. I try to keep the printing costs as low as possible, but in an emergency situation, there may be no electricity, cell service, or smartphone available. You won't lose your information if your smartphone gets stolen or breaks down. I made the print format as small as possible, used black and white where sufficient, and employed simple technologies for methods and tools on purpose.

A printed book is old-fashioned, but you can sell it, trade it in, or write notes in it—things you can't do with a digital format. Any author likes to sell their books for sure. But this is an honest tip that won't make me rich and won't make you poor, giving you maximum control over a situation where you need this information at hand.

Also, this project has been going on for a decade now. Expect me to update the content from time to time. Depending on when and where you got this copy, you may find some of the information outdated. Check for the latest editions in this case. I promise to keep adding and revising the content for years to come, God willing.

Until then, enjoy learning and keep an eye out for new titles from me coming up in the near future on Amazon.

Marcel A. Buth

Author

April 2023

www.ingramcontent.com/pod-product-compliance
Lightning Source LLC
Chambersburg PA
CBHW051547170526
45165CB00002B/919
* 9 7 8 1 4 8 2 3 4 5 3 3 9 *